Gently Into the Land
of the Meateaters

GENTLY INTO THE LAND
OF THE MEATEATERS

ESSAYS BY
JAMES SALLIS

Black Heron Press
Post Office Box 95676
Seattle, Washington 98145
http://mav.net/blackheron

ACKNOWLEDGMENTS

Thanks are extended to the editors of the publications in which these pieces first appeared:

"Old Story at Airport," "Standing By Death," "Seeing Ourselves," and "Living Without History" in the *Fort Worth Star-Telegram*, ©1984, 1985, 1987; "Gently into the Land of the Meateaters" in *Western Humanities Review*, ©1984; "Increments," "Demons & Mr. Cinq-Mars" and "Hearts of the City" in *Dallas Life*, ©1983, 1984, 1985; "Accounts Due" and "Revolutions" in *The Bloomsbury Review*, ©1986, 1987; "Cartons of Heartbreak" in *D Magazine*, ©1990; "One Sunday" in *The Texas Observer*, ©1987; "Literary Life" and "Temporary Life" in *Negative Capability*, ©1987, 1991; "Poetry: A Beginner's Manual" in *The Portland Review*, ©1989; "Where I Live" in *Fort Worth Quarterly*, ©1990; "Circles" in *Southwest Review*, ©1985; "American Solitude" in *North Dakota Quarterly*, ©1985; "Civility" in *America*, ©1984; "Taking the Stage" in *Karamu*, ©1996; and "Wounds of Waiting" in *Asylum Arts Annual*, ©1994. "Pushing Envelopes" and "Gone So Long" appear here for the first time.

Book Design: Ron Dakron and Jerome Gold
Cover Art and Design: Cami Lemke

Published by:
Black Heron Press
Post Office Box 95676
Seattle, Washington 98145
http://mav.net/blackheron

*To the memory of my father
and to Woodie*

TABLE OF CONTENTS

Old Story at Airport

It was very slowly that he came to realize his wife was an alcoholic.

For a long time other concerns — problems with her family, the first-year adjustments of any marriage, his solitary ways and offbeat attitudes — let them both evade the truth. Even her near-successful suicide attempt failed to drive the point home. Psychiatrists and social workers spoke a great deal about problems of living, unresolved resentments, anger turned inwards to fester as depression, but none of them picked up on her alcoholism.

Each morning she was herself again, loving, warm, open. But as the day went on, increasingly, she became someone else. She grew cold and argumentative, insisting upon her love for him one moment, slamming doors and attacking him verbally the next. Her eyes lost all light, her movements slowed. There were coordination problems.

Shortly after the wedding, she came home

from a visit with friends, sat in a chair, and fell forward onto her face. He left her there, and in the morning there were apologies, excuses, sorrow, anger. I've never done anything like that before, she told him. It would become a popular refrain.

Occasionally he'd return from work and find her gone. Once she came in at six, long after he'd picked up the girls, and slept slumped in a chair till early morning. Often she'd roll off the bed and spend the rest of the night on the floor, too flaccid, too without starch, for him to pull her back up. Then one morning he woke with her still in bed, and with wet sheets beneath them.

The explanations and apologies, the sorrow and anger continued. For days or weeks all would be well. Then he'd come into the kitchen and she'd gulp the glass of orange juice he reached for, or her fork would fall an inch or so to the right of the plate. One night she fell asleep in her chair in a favored restaurant.

Because they cared so much, they always covered things over, patched things back up. He carried his anger and resentments forward; she piled up new fears and new uncertainties as her self-respect crumbled.

He wanted only to have her as she was when they met, as she often still was, as she was most mornings still. She wanted him both to accept her as she was, and to save her.

Ten months after they were wed, in one of those impossible corners alcoholics work themselves into, she took an overdose of tranquilizers and spent several weeks in the hospital. He made the three-hour drive as often as he could, leaving the girls in the care of friends, exhausting what money they had left. Her passes were spent "talking things over" over drinks.

Patterns of anger and gentle reconciliation were set. Confessions passed back and forth. If I am sick, you must love me, she said. I will, he said, I do. You must forgive me. I will, he said, I do. Wonderful promises were made by both.

But things grew ever more difficult.

Because of the suicide attempt, there were numerous hearings, and eventually her parents received guardianship of the girls. A desperate relocation was followed by involuntary hospitalization. She returned home, stayed a while, then left to live with her parents until things there became so bad, after a month or so, that she was again hospitalized and, upon discharge, returned to him.

They talked endlessly, tiptoed around one another's feelings, tried to give one another "space" in the one-room apartment which was all they could afford.

Six months of AA meetings. Weeks of sobriety. Then he would find bottles hidden between boxes in the closet, on the far top of bathroom shelves, beneath nightstands. They'd quarrel and reconcile. Good days, bad days. He wished so badly that she didn't hurt so much. Some nights he would hold her and cry softly to himself long after she was asleep.

The waitress comes and refills our coffee cups. David is my oldest friend, though we've been out of touch, haven't seen one another in years. His pain lies on the table between us like a breathing thing. On his way to guest teaching, he's on layover, and I've come out to the airport. A red sunset billows down like a spent parachute beyond plate glass. Two 747s scream soundlessly down the runway towards us.

How's she doing now? I ask him of the younger wife I haven't met.

I don't know, Jim.

He sips coffee and looks out at the runway, the reddening sky, passengers at the end of journeys.

A week ago, he says, she disappeared from the apartment and went to a bar. She's called twice and is staying with someone she met there. She says that she's okay but just can't come back right now, and that she loves me more than anything in the world.

David's not mentioned love before this, but at that moment it shows in his eyes brighter than the sun outside, hard and purposeful as the jets streaming towards us, impossible as heavier-than-air flight.

GENTLY INTO THE LAND
OF THE MEATEATERS

They are all listening to a record. Schoenberg.
The fiddles take ideas, wrap them in wood, throw
them into the air where they strike and grate
against others. There is a tremendous energy, and
at the same time a certain stolidness, to this music.
Outside, the sun hangs on the sky like a boil. They
sit facing a long corridor at the end of which they
see sometimes, as through a reversed telescope or
stereopticon, the faces of people they know
bringing them magazines or jigsaw puzzles. They
are supposed to relate this music, these people who
can fit no two things together anymore, or for
whom everything has locked into place with no
room left over, to the craft or activity (sewing,
potholders, lanyards) in which they are engaged.

I am here because odd seams have sprung
open in the sky and will not close.

Emerson tells us that wherever we go, whatever
we do, self is the sole object we study and learn.
Certainly each of us becomes a metaphor of the

world: we figure the world from ourselves. But
we may forget this is only metaphor and end trying
to balance the whole world on our nose, like a seal
with a globe. And when belief in external reality
collapses, the mind feeds on itself. Here sundered,
sovereign worlds wander through the same closed
sky, occasionally (but not often) colliding.

It is Robert Lowell I keep coming back to, his
"locked razors" and the description of Murder
Incorporated's Czar Lepke:

> Flabby, bald, lobotomized
> he drifted in a sheepish calm,
> where no agonizing reappraisal
> jarred his concentration on the electric chair—
> hanging like an oasis in his air
> of lost connections . . .

Perry sits for hours with his foot on the table,
sunk into his chair before the TV, always the same
chair, not moving until it is time for meals, for
group, for OT, meds, bed. Perry is a chemist,
committed by his parents following a suicide
attempt. Once as we are walking to the gym for a
film about Hawaii, he comes up beside me to say
that he is just waiting out his time, that he will kill
himself when he is released. I know of no other
occasion when he spoke to anyone on the ward.

At night the walls lean towards me. I see in
clouds the eyes of whales. I write that shadows

perform and stand around me clapping, that the trees grow smaller, the flowers every day more threatening now. Of the purple knife-edge in damaged hands. I write: *I lift the cup, I am burning up.*

Our days proceed like those of Fifties' school-children, dull and featureless as the buildings and walkways through which we move. We march together to the cafeteria, square-dancing lessons with horribly scratched records, ancient travelogue films, a talent show. Three times a day we queue at the nurse's station for medications. At dawn those scheduled for shock are assembled in the dayroom and escorted through trees to a small grey building. They return to us stunned, suspended in an endless present, the clear fluid of their synapses turned to milk.

In the afternoon we are left alone. The long hours stretch out like a barren plain from the TV set where everyone huddles, as about a campfire. Most days I sit alone in a line of chairs at one side of the room with a book of Chekhov's stories. Later I learn that this is duly noted in my chart: I do not participate in ward activities.

An amazing person comes among us, a Cajun who takes over the coffee room, scouring and organizing it down to the last cup and spoon, forever brewing huge pots of coffee into which milk sinks helplessly. Next he attacks the ward floors with a polisher. In such exercise of will, and in this company, he and the knots of muscle in his arms are one: nests of potency, intensity. Like a child he is eager to please. Sometimes at night he strums a guitar and keens old country songs.

Here, as elsewhere and always, I stand apart, watching. This is what an artist does—he looks, he tries to see—and what I had slowly unlearned. In the privacy of my life and art by degrees I had folded in upon myself, a closing hand. Nor did the unfolding begin there in the hospital's close spaces; I had only the sense that soon it would.

Because we are sick we cannot be well. Every action or attitude is interpreted in light of our supposed sickness: Conrad's quite reasonable anger at the patronizing behavior of the nursing staff vanishes into rococo vagaries of analysis; my own solitary ways and disinclination for chatter are surely pathological. We have become self-fulfilling prophecy. One morning I choose not to shave; during the day I am questioned about this by the ward nurse, my assigned social worker and a staff physician.

We are told on the one hand to express ourselves, that we must vent our feelings to survive, yet receive clearly the message that we must not disrupt in any way the effortless, level roll of ward routine — conflicting information not unlike that delivered by the larger society beyond our locked doors. I recall the common history, among schizophrenics, of parents who insist upon truths in direct conflict with what the child actually sees.

It is summer. In sharp contrast to our own lethargies, flies rocket about the rooms and rebound from the walls. One afternoon in the doldrums between lunch and dinner I begin counting them. Fifty-eight.

For so arcane and recondite a body of theory, treatment is astonishingly mechanistic, as though we are simple toys that have broken. Bombed to the ground with chemicals, we are led into groups and encouraged to talk, to "share" our problems, fears, failures. Ambrose Bierce said the only thing anyone could ever do with good advice was to give it to someone else, quickly. Whenever there's a lull the social worker says, And how do you *feel* about that? Four years after all this, a friend who is mending as I mended writes that she rarely gets past the first aisle at the supermarket, stunned by such diversity and choice. I can't decide what deodorant to buy, she tells me, and here I'm supposed to be making life decisions.

And poetry, of course, if it fails to make the world large again, does nothing.

The doctors pass among us at rare intervals, alternately annoyed that we remain ill and demanding of their time; defensive that they are of little help; or simply frightened. For the most part they are residents, putting in their time, paying dues, inclined to accede pro forma to the ward nurse's often questionable clinical observations and suggestions. But while among them I encounter Dr. Ball, who seems very young and speaks to me kindly, intelligently, after shaking my hand, the only one to do so. He asks to read my book, which has just come out. Once when my medication is reduced sharply and I feel the ends of my nerves fraying like ropes about to let go, like evergreens all inside me (I'd not been told of the change), he comes to the ward at 3 a.m., though he is not on call, to reassure me.

Much of our treatment and activity seeks to establish among us a sense of community. In some ways this is successful, though perhaps not as intended. Marx's catechism of oppression, despotism and epochal struggle might commend itself, in this surround, to the most conservative among us. My own inchoate communism, though forever wounded by an unshakable faith in the importance of the individual, flourishes here and returns with me intact to the world outside. At night the glass nurse's station with its pure light seems a great ship pushing its way through the dark, a sentry post, a fortress.

Gene is a burned-out relic of the Sixties who still observes the forms of the time (long hair, sandals, beads, slang) like an emigrant preserving his culture in the new land. He cannot maintain his vegetarianism here; the vegetables are cooked with meat or seasoned with lard, and complementary proteins are infrequent. He tries to fill himself with beans, rice, lettuce and milk, gesturing while in line (generally to no avail) for extra portions, pushing the scraps of meat aside from his cabbage or carrots. He cannot or will not talk, and appears largely out of touch. I am told by an orderly (I do not know if this is true) that he killed his wife and children.

You must understand that this is a place of high intention. This is a city where they mend torn sails, or souls; hammer hearts back into place; make fine adjustments in the eye; replace the mind's printed circuits. Where they roll the projector lens slowly till all the blurred, shapeless forms snap into focus.

But it is also an insupportably mean, petty place, just as the unswept dark corners of our hearts are mean and petty, with hard grey floors, bare walls, windows that will not open. It is every army barracks that ever held recruits, every tough schoolyard or gym, every ghetto, prison, deadend street. Some light must always shine behind our lives; here it is very difficult for that light to get through. The language has a long memory: because we are patients, we bear our pain and trials calmly, without complaint.

The game played on this grey court, as in the world outside, is control — here, though, with little regard for pretense and with the absolute sanction of our illness; recusants simply confirm established debilities. We are the poor through bourgeois eyes: if we are sick, surely it is because we intend to be. Joey is confined to the dayroom, dressed only in pajamas, for failing to get the "phonecard" (a square of cardboard attached to a keychain) before making a call at the pay station in the hall just outside the ward.

One morning a recent arrival comes out of the coffee room with an arm full of cups and begins heaving them into the window. George, he says: Irene, Truth, Love. A week or so later, at 9 p.m., another begins sobbing loudly and weeps for two days without stop.

There is a great evil pushing at the world in each of us, and it needs but a small slipway, an opening. We who cannot keep a tune want to move the stars to pity with our voices. From our mothers' ponderous bellies we pass of a sudden, and then very slowly, into this harsh land. Suns flare and die above us; all is awash with yellow light. The voices of others come to us across the plain. We live on water. We *are* water.

In my final week I finish Chekhov and begin *Notes from the Underground*, which goes with me back into the world.

On the long drive home (like airports, state hospitals are built away from urban centers) I begin to realize again how large the world is, how disorganized, how various. The first lines of Wallace Stevens' "Connoisseur of Chaos" come to me:

A. A violent order is disorder; and
B. A great disorder is an order. These
Two things are one. (Pages of illustrations.)

Years later I clip from the *Times Herald* a cartoon by P. Kolsti that shows a man cringing under a chair, his own huge brain, his own mind, hovering in the air above. It remains on the wall by my desk.

For several days I sit on my patio, reading sometimes, but mostly watching the procession of people, traffic, animals, light, wind, rain. This is what the artist does, I tell myself. He looks; he tries to see. The weather swings wildly from hot

to cold. There are patterns everywhere, but the
world remains unreadable as a walnut. In a book
on French literature I find this quote from Rilke:

> It submerges us. We organize it.
> It falls to pieces. We organize it
> again and fall to pieces ourselves.

Somehow, it all seems to end there.

Increments

"Father, the dark moths
Crouch at the sills of earth, waiting."
—James Wright

On the wall of my study is a poster with a sad little guy holding a no smoking sign. His pear-shaped nose overhangs the sign, his eyes are round and black as wells, a single strand of hair sprouts from his head like a weed. It was drawn by a nineteen-year-old named Debbie who died three years ago. For a long time after her death I sat here and tried to write about her, what she had meant to me, and couldn't. It was all over—the suction canisters burned, the crying done—but I could not get it outside myself. I remember telling my daughter the next day as I took her to school, able to say only: Debbie is dead. Probably there's no one else who thinks of Debbie much now, after these three years.

She had cystic fibrosis, a congenital disease with severe pulmonary replications, and though she was nineteen, the disease's toll was such that she was not much larger than my eight-year-old daughter. Debbie knew she would die from CF, as had so many of the older cystics, all her friends, in the year I knew her, and we often talked about how death would come, whether she would know. Early one evening a few months before her own death she called from the hospital to tell me that Sonya had just died: "I thought you would want to know." I thanked her, and we said no more. Several times she spoke to me of her dread at someday waking and finding her family there with her in the hospital room, knowing only then and by that, that this time she would die.

In the last week of her life the family began gathering. The twenty-year-old aunt and uncle she lived with, her stepfather who had remarried following her mother's death, her father whom she had not seen for many years. She did not speak of her old dread now. And when she called me that Sunday, it was not to talk (for she had little enough breath remaining) but to tell me, without words, that she would not see me again. I said that I would be in the next day. But by nine o'clock it was too late. When I arrived at the hospital in bright sunshine, the room was empty, the trashcans full. She had gone quietly two hours before, slipping over that final sill.

It is altogether fitting that Debbie should have passed so quietly away from us. She was always soft-spoken, shy, carrying with her a strange solitude and inner calm to which but a few of us were admitted. I know that she never spoke to me of her disease with the anger and rage one expected; instead, her delight in life signaled itself constantly. She once described for me in great detail her Christmas shopping — incredibly stressful for her, but that was not the part I heard. When I took her to dinner on pass from the hospital, she ate for perhaps fifteen minutes, excused herself, went into the bathroom to throw up, then came back and resumed eating: she would not let her pleasure be abridged. With the graduation announcement that represented amazing perseverance in the face of her increasing illness, she enclosed a torn-off corner of notebook paper with "Sorry, Jim, I'm too lazy to write" scribbled across it.

But her life, of course, *was* abridged, in ways and to degrees only the chronically ill can understand. It was a slow, painful shrinking: grey formed at the borders of her life and day after day crept ever closer, shutting away more and more, inexorably diminishing her. There was no drama to it — just the relentless procession of days. It was not hubris or divine flaw, not quarreling, capricious gods, but the disease that crushed her: something inside her, part of her. Increasingly towards the end the disease *was* her. And yet she remained concerned about the feelings of her family and those about her, those taking care of her. Debbie wanted so badly not to hurt anyone, *to join*.

She was nineteen: I keep returning to that. And she was excluded from every community but that of her disease, a member of the CF family, of children's hospital regulars. Hospital staff for the most part treated her little differently from cystics who were ten or twelve, as though physical size and maturity were correlative. But even in casual conversation she proved remarkably glib and intelligent, and those of us who chose to look further found at her center a clear sense of self. Chronically ill children, at least in part due to the disproportionate time spent among adults, often evidence a maturity beyond their years, almost as though in such a small room the furniture must be set up right away.

Debbie summoned herself, quite naturally it seemed, towards goals. When I first met her, even with extended hospitalizations, that goal was to graduate from high school, from (as she would say) a *regular* high school. It became difficult then for her to find workable goals, and a kind of gentle fantasy appeared. She spoke of becoming a veterinary assistant, of moving to Dallas and taking a job. She even applied for clerical work at the hospital where she was treated, though the personnel office there refused to take her application seriously and put her off as one would a child, failing to grant her even the dignity of straightforward response. Plans were eventually made that she would come here and live with Sharon, a respiratory therapist, and Kathy, another teenage cystic. Debbie went off to her aunt's for a final visit. Several weeks passed without word from her. Then one night at eleven or twelve my phone rang. She was coming back to the hospital, quite ill. My wife met the plane (I had to work) and after waiting for some time following debarkation, finally inquired about Debbie—who had passed out in flight. The next time my phone rang late at night it was Debbie's aunt I spoke to; Debbie could manage only a few words. This was her last visit, her last flight.

In those final months Debbie continued to resent being treated as a child, and increasingly she voiced her resentment. In the hospital this had as much to do with the habits of the staff as with her size; it was, after all, a children's hospital, and the average age of our patients was probably four or five. Once she had gone to a general hospital but, depressed by "old men with catheters," never returned there. I often recall a time at the airport when Debbie was flying back to Amarillo. The ticket clerk had routinely asked who would be meeting the young lady. The young lady, I responded, is 19 years old and responsible for herself. There was a brief, politic pause while the clerk (probably not much over nineteen herself) looked down at Debbie, then a nod.

A more serious complaint towards the end concerned infringements of privacy. She realized that intimate details of her life were known or readily accessible to anyone about the hospital, a terrible burden for anyone but particularly for a 19-year-old girl, and in her final year grew to resent the continued trespass of well-intentioned staff (social workers, interns or psychiatrists in training) with their biased questions, judgements, advice, curiosity. Debbie felt that she had been subjected to that long enough already and had contributed sufficiently to the education of America's future healthcare pros. Finally she refused to receive any staff aside from the resident attending her case, her regular nurses, and respiratory therapists such as myself who administered her hour-long treatments four times a day. In those habits of thought peculiar

to hospitals, where virtually any act of indepen-
dence or self-assertion is automatically considered
symptomatic of psychological illness or (that
wonderful nonce word) "maladjustment," Debbie's
refusal was discussed widely, taking on ever more
baroque avatars and interpretations. But like
Bartleby she had said "I would prefer not to," and
could not be budged.

We knew that Debbie had come back to us to
die. We sensed the motion of those dark moths
beyond the sill. Miles had become inches. But we
went on talking, when we talked, of the usual
things: how her aunt took her Medicaid payments
for room and board and was reluctant to give
Debbie even a few dollars of it (it was small
enough, anyway) for clothes; how she slept on
the couch there and didn't even have a place for
the machine she used each day for breathing
treatments; the taste that always came to her (like
an epileptic's aura) three or four days before she
became seriously ill.

If there were a photograph here of Debbie —
and sadly I have none — it would show long,
lustrous black hair; small breasts; smooth, beautiful
skin with something of the cystic's translucence to
it; soulful brown eyes. It would not show, or would
show but slightly, the barreled chest and clubbed

fingers she also shared with them, or the ravaged teeth. Debbie would be there; the disease would not be.

Nor would that photograph show the way her skin looked the last time I saw her, grey and dull like smoke, like tarnished silver. *She's so small*, I thought as I hugged her—something I'd never really thought of, never sensed, before that time. She was barely conscious, coming to for brief periods after her treatments, then sinking back into torpor. Her shoulders heaved with the effort of breathing; veins pulsed at her neck. But even with such massive effort she gained little air. A moth, I thought then, would barely tremble from her breath: such a tiny tide.

Of course we all live finally in Zeno's land, proceeding by increments and never arriving, while from the other side of this tissue-thin sky come crashing, with the least tear, the eternal oceans of darkness. Debbie's was simply a far more visible, far less metaphoric form of the ticking death we all play host to, that eats its way out of us, as from a cocoon. I sometimes think of her as the girl in de Chirico's "Melancholy and Mystery of the Street," rolling her hoop towards those brooding enigmas. And I have wanted for three years now to set down here something of Debbie's gentle grace and character, something too of the faltering motions of memory. To retain what I could of her. You have to understand: someone very special has been removed from this world, and the world is diminished because of it. I have to believe that. But of course "the world" (our word for everything we know and don't) is not likely to notice, or care.

On another wall of my study there's a drawing of a huge eagle sweeping down from the sky, *filling* the sky, talons black and big as mountains. Before him, beneath him, stands a mouse. The mouse's legs are braced and he has raised his right hand towards that eagle, middle finger extended. The legend reads: Courage in the Face of Adversity.

Demons and Mr. Cinq-Mars

In our later years, having become largely what we *will* become, it is not uncommon, particularly if one is by nature reflective, to look back on the people and events of our life with some intent towards understanding which have been important, which have helped deliver us to the very shores from which we now survey them.

Our parents, certainly. The place and circumstances of our birth and early years. For me, an older brother who brought Aristotle and George Bernard Shaw to me from the great world beyond — who brought so very *many* things from that distant place. Our teachers.

More and more now, as brash young springs chase tired old winters down the hill and away again and again, I realize that a man I've thought of but rarely is central to my life.

His name was Robert J. Cinq-Mars, and I first saw him the day I, a sixth-grader, walked into the band room of an old four-story brick schoolhouse in the small Southern town where I was born, with a silver trumpet underarm as aged and battered as the building itself. He was new that year. Canadian, I suppose, from the name. After all these years I have only dim memories of just how he looked, snapshots faded with time. I seem to remember a mobile, expressive face which appeared, even in laughter, to form itself about some round and unyielding sadness, black-rimmed glasses, a longish flattop. He always wore suits with white shirts and ties, I believe, never sportcoats; perhaps it was always the same suit.

In that band room on the top floor we would count 1-2-3-4 and blow our terribly untuned horns. Within weeks, it seems now (but in reality far longer), I was copying themes of TV shows like *Zorro*, writing down valve-fingerings in place of the notation I couldn't yet manage. About the same time, my brother began bringing me records when he came home from college on holidays or for the summer — the Brandenburgs, the Mozart horn concerti and G-minor, Wagner, the Eroica, Mahler's First — all of which, scarred with age and much use, I still have. Soon, too, I was in awe of Mr. Cinq-Mars. For he was more than a band director: he was, rumor had it, a composer.

I should explain that these were the days I first came to my own vocation. I had begun writing

stories on endless sheets of memo paper, even
drew a series of cartoons (though I was far more
interested in the captions) for my classmates.
Generally these were adapted from what I was
reading, but I took the basic idea or situation only,
developing from that my own plots and reversals.
Even this early I realized that the principle utility
of literature was the making of further literature.

I suppose Mr. Cinq-Mars must have been the
first creative person I'd known, so different in my
youthful mind from the salesmen, store clerks and
farmers around me, so much more like a figure
from the books I somehow saw as offering an
alternative to, rather than a reflection of, life.

The town itself had been important in older
days: a major harbor when the Mississippi was
the world's longest trade road, a crucial strong-
hold during the Civil War (there remains a fine
Confederate cemetery always awash, it seems, in
fallen magnolia leaves), a major crossroad in the
itineraries of bluesmen like Robert Johnson and
Sonny Boy Williamson in the Thirties and Forties.
Now it existed only because it *had been* important;
all life was gone from it and, contracting about
itself, closing up, it had become petty and mean-
spirited. In one small section of town sat the
sculptured yards and clapboard castles of the

town's rich, rightful descendants of oldtime plantation owners; in row after row across the road from my own home stretched the tarpaper shacks generations of Negro families kept filled. When the city finally passed an ordinance requiring indoor toilets (this was in the late Fifties, I think), toilets were installed where closest to sewer lines—in kitchens, bedrooms, closets, perhaps even on porches. You will not be too greatly surprised, I'm certain, to learn that the owner of these hovels lived in one of the clapboard castles and had the most elegantly sculptured yard of all. Nor will it surprise you to learn that when I first came to Marx, many years later, those shacks sprang at once, irrevocably, into my memory.

Mr. Cinq-Mars lived in a converted garage behind someone's house. I saw it once on a Saturday morning, going over to pick up keys to the band room. I had formed a quartet for which I did arrangements (French horn, violin, bassoon and saxophone: a curious ensemble) and we needed our instruments for rehearsal. Where are you getting your music? he asked, emerging from the kitchen looking more rumpled than usual. I told him that I was writing it and he looked at me as though recognizing something for the first time. He said nothing. I don't know what he felt for me then, pleasure or sympathy; sometimes I wonder.

Gradually his arrangements, meticulously written out by hand and copied on the first Xerox I'd seen, began finding their way to our music stands. He had added many instruments, particularly low reeds such as bass and alto clarinets, rather unusual at the time, to fill out the lower end of the band so that it had become orchestra-like, and his arrangements (we soon played *only* his arrangements) were written to our specific instrumentation. Among these was an arrangement of the 1812 Overture we later played onstage in Chicago, though under another director, for Mr. Cinq-Mars was gone by then. It was this arrangement, in fact, which had caused us to be invited to the nationwide showcase for high school bands. I've a recording of the concert we gave there (to which I am listening just now), and another disc (possibly the one submitted to Chicago) featuring a fluffed note (yes, mine) in the horn-led intro. The latter contains, also, an original composition by Mr. Cinq-Mars.

He brought these in periodically. Everyone had heard the story: that he'd prayed only to be allowed to compose music, to be given that talent, and that in turn he would not make any commercial use of that music, never publish it, never sell it — a curious reversal of the usual Paganini/devil-pact tale and surely (one assumes) apocryphal. Yet there was something in his gentleness and unprepossessing manner which leads me to believe there was in the tale some core of truth. In fact he seemed to have no ego at all, only a calm assurance of his abilities, and suddenly now, as I write, it comes to me that he was round-shouldered and concave, as though shaped around something very hard and important at his center, or as though trying to protect himself from blows. He spoke rapidly and in a low voice — sometimes it was difficult to make out what he said from the podium — and especially when meeting parents, seemed quite shy. His head would dip lower, his voice sink, he would watch the floor, waiting for this to be over.

I suppose now that all his free time was spent at the kitchen table in his converted garage writing out the arrangements that gained so much attention for our band and copying out all the parts himself, transposing as he went. There was such a profusion of material it could not have been otherwise. Yet one evening as he dropped me at my house (we often had lengthy after-school rehearsals, and I was one of perhaps nine kids he'd ferried home afterwards in his old blue station wagon) he said, as I reached for my horn, to just leave it there, I must have a lot of other things I needed to do. Music's not everything, he said; you have to get away from it sometimes.

He vanished in the summer between my junior and senior years. I attended band camp that summer, and several weeks before the end of school Mr. Cinq-Mars had surprised me with a beautiful silver double-horn, an Olds. Towards the end of camp I was told that someone would retrieve the horn the last day; I was to meet him in the cafeteria. I don't remember who came to take the horn, but whoever it was, told me that Mr. Cinq-Mars would not be returning in the fall. None of us ever knew why; to this day I don't know.

From the beginning Mr. Cinq-Mars was said to be homosexual, or "queer" as it was always put in those days, and there were daily stories (always from the macho types, it seems) of attempted seductions and a lurid past, terrible jokes for which his name served as punch line or prelude. And so, quite inevitably, the story began making its way around that he'd been picked up by police, always in some mythical far-flung location such as Michigan, in the midst of propositioning some young man, or worse. He may well have been homosexual, and for all I know something like this could in fact be the circumstance that bore him away from us. It could have been simply the narrowness of that small town, the simple fact that he did not, could not, would not fit. There were other rumors of gross irresponsibility (I was not the only recipient of a new instrument), and of madness. I know that I felt a terrible, personal sense of loss.

Years later other music — the blues in particular, but various ethnic and folk musics — would become as important to me as classical. I would quit playing horn in college finally, but would teach myself guitar and then several other stringed instruments. I would teach these instruments and write about them extensively. And everywhere I would go in this world, from a walkup flat off Portobello Road in London to a psychiatric hospital even deeper in the mythic American South, music would go along, as inseparable a part of my life as breath itself, as water, as sunlight. It would bear me through many difficult years, past a hundred mouths that nipped at my life, and other times would alone express for me a sense of joy, beauty and belonging that else would have remained in me inchoate.

I did not know all this then, of course. I knew only that someone important to me was gone forever, spirited away in another of those inscrutable cosmic disjunctions which increasingly seemed to me (and seem still) the way of our world.

Another director came that fall, a worldly, powerful man of strong temper and voice, the kind for whom you could not imagine anything ever going wrong, a winner. He drove a Buick and lived in a house. Under his direction (and with new arrangements) we went on to Chicago, sounding like nothing more than just another high school band. Because the demon was out of the bottle now, you see; it was empty.

I wonder where the demon is, and what has happened to him in all these years since he gave me the single thread that has stitched together my own difficult, often disjunctive life.

I am writing this in a converted garage in a small Texas town, looking out the window at my twelve-year-old truck (my father's before he died in that same Southern town) and trying to recover from the crumbling of a second marriage at age thirty-nine. I sometimes go for days without speaking to anyone; at night wind works its way in through diverse cracks and faults, moaning in close harmony, slow Gregorian chants.

The most important lessons are those we do not know we are giving. Working at this essay I've frequently paused to shut off the typewriter and listen to music from the radio or phonograph — Saint-Saëns's "The Swan," Beethoven symphonies, the first Strauss horn concerto, Charles Ives, Chopin — and certainly I shall always be thankful to Mr. Cinq-Mars for the music he gave me, the sense of what it is, what it can be (and so what we ourselves might be). But there's far more to my gratitude, for I also learned from him for the first time (a lesson oft-repeated in later years) what it is to be an artist, the dedication and the single-mindedness that alone will allow you to survive. I learned that *making* art, the process itself, was important, and not what became of it. And I learned a great deal as well about intolerance and small towns; about what it means to be a teacher; about being an individual, following one's own path, in this cluttered, conspiring world. I learned something very important about solitude.

I cannot think that his years have been any easier than my own, but I hope that they have been. I hope that music is still there beside him, and will always be, even when there is little else.

Artists are only people who watch and listen intently, who try to understand and then, knowing always they will fail, try to tell what it is they've seen and heard. Probably Robert J. Cinq-Mars has forgotten the small town he departed abruptly and the bookish trumpet player he switched to French horn. Yet I hope he knows that sometime, somewhere, at least one of us *watched,* one of us *listened,* one of us was helped by him to become truly human.

ACCOUNTS DUE:
SELF-PORTRAIT AT FORTY-TWO

He turned forty-two last month, on a day that came and went largely unnoticed. His several children, as the blues song goes, are way out in the world somewhere. Most days now, he wears an oversize sweatshirt and jeans, sitting at the sole window in the one-room apartment he and his wife share. The typewriter and radio on the table before him have followed him through most of his adult life. He drinks tea incessantly.

In the time of that life, and in his work, he has been many people, and if sometimes he contradicted himself well then, like Whitman he contains multitudes.

For a few years there he was Dylan Thomas, a doomed minor poet. Then in quick succession a blues musician, political radical, expatriate editor, science fiction star. He tried very hard for a number of years to become French. He turned himself, almost, into a madman. He was Tolstoy for a time, dressing in workshirts and jeans to embrace the moral life at whatever cost. Then tried on the habit of gentleman essayist.

None of the clothes fit, and now he is back to his own irredeemable, baggy ones.

He writes small essays about his life for local papers and magazines. Two or three novels tumble about in the out-trays of New York publishers. Every few months he receives an award for some poem or story which appeared in a literary magazine read only by its other contributors. Young writers periodically write to tell him how important his work has been to their own.

Many of the things he will not do or become in his life are clear now, and he supposes that this is what life's journey consists of, this gradual giving-up of ground, a quiet acceptance of could-have-beens. He wishes he could believe there was a gain for every loss, but that sort of thinking, common to moralists and Christians, is alien to him.

He has believed deeply in art and in women. Both have damned, and saved, his life.

Daily long walks take him among the parks and recreation centers of affluent Arlington, along Marrow Bone Springs where Indians once lived, and among the homeless poor of Fort Worth. Once he lived as close to the ground as these latter, half-humorously suggesting that all decision makers be required to live for six months without money or resources on the streets of a major city. Once he was locked away for a time, and it changed him forever.

Once a revolutionary of sorts, he now believes that authority exists only to be rebelled against, a ceaseless dialectic that must just go on and on, sea tearing at beach, beach pushing against sea.

And so he carries his heroes (Voltaire, Marx, Woody Guthrie, Pasternak and Pushkin, Thoreau), changed by it all, like himself, into middle age.

He carries, also, stacks of escalating debts, unanswered letters, cardboard boxes of old and abandoned manuscripts. He carries forward the unfinished books on the table and floor about him and the familiar weight of those others, every year more and more, as yet unbegun. They simply accumulate, insubstantial as clouds.

He remembers a wholly negative description Emerson once wrote of Thoreau — that he ate no meat, that he owned nothing, that he neither drank nor smoked, belonged to no group — and wonders if Bartleby's "I would prefer not to" may not be a central metaphor of America. Certainly his own life has seemed a kind of retreat, a ceaseless decamping and resettling, reformulated again and again like America itself, like Whitman's ongoing revisions of *Leaves of Grass*. He has a predilection for solitude and early mornings alone.

Now he thinks, *this* morning, of other wives and lives. He has been loved. In a letter to a friend he writes: Will we ever recover from this terrible ache, from these words wanting eternally to be born in us? Must we know all our lives this wanting, these hollows?

Today birds have overtaken the power lines, and one sits on the narrow ledge of his window turning its teardrop head to watch him at his work. With the very pulse and presence of living things, Bach plays on the radio beside him.

Rain in the sky, but shy about falling.

With a shock of recognition, as the bird flies away, an old thought comes to him. He thinks how, in all these endless pages, all these stories and poems and essays and letters, he tries to give imaginary meaning to parts of his life he doesn't understand.

He thinks how, once, he understood so clearly.

Pushing Envelopes

I wonder sometimes, as I stuff yet another perfectly innocent envelope with return postage, or tear one open to find my manuscript bearing the hoofprint of the paper clip holding a form rejection to its bosom, whether this is not a silly thing for a fifty-three-year-old, supposedly professional writer to be doing.

It's been habit, of course, for a long time now. Like Baudelaire's vampire, whose bones after the metamorphosis go on creaking like a signboard in the wind. Or, again, as in Apollinaire:

> Their hearts are like their doors
> Always doing business

The doors swing to and fro with distressing regularity. Stories and poems and essays wrapped up warmly in their best new clothes and sent out the door—like the boll weevil, jus' lookin' for a home—come back bringing along unwelcome friends, sad little notes that read Try us again! or invitations to subscribe at special rates.

Ah, another great Sallis story," a friend said

just last year upon seeing something of mine in a magazine. I pointed out that the story had swum valiantly upstream 54 times before finally lodging in a bend. My record of submissions filled both sides of an index card. I'd spent $69.12 on postage alone, never mind the cost of manila envelopes, photocopies and paper. In return I received two copies of the magazine.

It doesn't even feel good when you stop, as in the old joke. Every few years I *do* stop. Tuck little orphan stories away in a shelter somewhere, find a nice spot for homeless poems under a bridge, and swear never again. But before long I catch myself sneaking to the corner mailbox with a plain brown envelope, or get caught slipping out of the house with a stack of submissions under my coat on a coolish 98-degree July evening.

Now, to secure all that money for postage, manila envelopes, photocopies and paper, I write books for which I get paid reasonably well, or reviews for the likes of *Book World* and the *Los Angeles Times*. Those who read my books aren't likely to come across, even to know about, stories appearing in *Straw Dog Quarterly* or *Dead Horse Review*, or to care about poems appearing anywhere. Even my book editors have little interest in this other, subterranean life. Questioned by authorities, they disavow all knowledge of the "second gentleman" staying with the good Dr. J. Luckily (thus far at least) I've always managed to get home, drink the antidote and change back in time.

So just w hy *is* it that I go on shoveling good money and fair-to-middling effort into such enterprise, sending out stories and poems to publications likely to be seen only by other contributors? (Note that I do not say *read* by other contributors.) Reputation? I've had mine, such as it is, for years now, like a pair of old jeans; it's unlikely to be much affected by a poem buried among dozens of others in *Driftword* or *Wormturn,* or by a two-page story in *Elephant Hump* stating that its author needs no introduction. But I *do* go on, like some out-of-control, perpetual-motion existentialist making his leap into faith, nostrils pinched shut with finger and thumb, again and again. When recently a friend offered his definition of *crazy* as "doing the same thing over and over, expecting different results," I cringed.

Maybe more than anything (this just occurred to me, go with me on it for a moment) it has to do with getting the little buggers out of house and mind for a while. Ghosts, once-beloved pets gone blind and incontinent with age, bunions or heel blisters: choose your metaphor. They're always there; they don't go away. But if you work at it, you can get temporary relief. Hand the kids a few dollars and tell them to go take in a matinee, buying your ticket to a little peace.

Truth to tell (though I have to confess that my favorite title for a book about writing is *Telling Lies for Fun and Profit*), I don't even know what to call the things anymore. Little magazines? Well, lots of them make pretty good door stops these days. Literary magazines? Sure . . . if you're in the habit of calling your pants trousers and got reared instead of raised — in which case the word is pronounced *lit'ry*. Increasingly, even among book readers and interviewers, I find myself having to describe these publications. Your basic show-and-tell situation. Remembering all the time Louis Armstrong saying of jazz that if you had to ask, you weren't going to understand the answer.

Not only don't I know what to call these publications, I have no idea where they fit in anymore, what function they might serve. Where, on the bus of a nation whose conversation and very mythology come from last night's sitcoms and movies, does a magazine filled with knickknacks of poetry, essays and short fiction find a seat? Most nowadays seem vaguely proprietary, attached in one way or another to university writing programs, the intellectual-property equivalent of corporate newsletters. There's a sameness to them, never stronger than in those most adamantly transgressive, a flattening-out that admittedly may have as much to do with my own age as with intrinsic quality.

We thought we were doing important work. I remember. We thought literature was important and would always be, that it offered us maps to find our way to new worlds. Now we just go on overbuilding the world we have, and the maps lie in shreds around us. Publishing has become a kind of demi-intellectual garment district, with runners pushing racks of clothes everywhere in the street, obstructing traffic and getting in good people's ways.

And literature?

Years ago I wrote a piece for *American Pen* suggesting that, abandoned by mainstream publishing, our literature — even then we'd begun to miss it, you see, and to go looking — had fled to these magazines. Like those remote islands in science fiction upon which prehistoric life has survived into the present. Now I don't know *where* it's gone. I've looked. I can't find it. If anyone's seen it recently, please call. I'll pay for information, photos, confirmed sightings.

Always we believed, those historical magazines and historical me, in literature's adversary intent: that literature necessarily sets itself against prevailing currents — the received wisdom and assumptions of our time. Frost might be right that "We can't appraise the time in which we act," but by God we were gonna try. We were meant, as writers, to be outlaws, hired guns, eternal outsiders, long riders. We didn't light out for the territory, we planned on hauling the territory behind us, right back to civilization.

Maybe these days when I slip these manuscripts, these stories and poems and essays, into envelopes, maybe, more than anything else I'm doing, I'm reminding myself of all that. What it felt like to believe that literature and the people who create it are important. That we might change things. Maybe it helps this one over-civilized, over-comfortable, housebroken writer sustain the illusion that he's still out there with dust and starlight in his face, far away from all the Aunt Sallies and all the compromises, out there where there are no fences and anything, *anything*, can happen.

Cartons of Heartbreak

1.

Staring deeply into my eyes she told me, "I put your number in the Rolodex today."

Not quite the declaration of undying love I'd hoped for — something along the lines of "I've waited for you all my life," perhaps — but with age, our perspective on these things changes. We become either more desperate or calmer. More desperate didn't seem humanly possible, so I was working on calm.

And for Susan, even though, as she pointed out, leaves were forever falling from that Rolodex never to be seen again, inclusion therein was signal.

Nevertheless, it *was* autumn. Months later, as I sat on my porch pondering Katherine Mansfield's statement of one of the chief benefits of solitude — "Even if I should, by some awful chance, find a hair upon my bread and honey, at any rate it is my own hair" — it occurred to me that as time goes on

I am going through companions at an ever faster, rather alarming rate.

Of course, one gets over it all a lot faster, too. This time, for instance, I was up and about, just as though nothing had happened, by the following spring. I walked into my kitchen and into a largely unacknowledged problem of the single life.

Paul Tillich said that the history of religion is a graveyard of dead symbols. My *histoire d'amour*, I realized, was a litter of drinks and foodstuffs I'd never use. Cabinets, shelves and refrigerator were filled with them.

There were, for example, four cans of diet chocolate drink which Susan was drinking when I first met her. Naturally I'd gone out and stocked up on it. As I recall, she lost her taste for this drink shortly before losing her taste for me, and the cans had languished there ever since.

One cabinet shelf was lined with herb teas another companion drank. For almost a month my apartment hosted innumerable half-cups of this tea. I'd find them, abandoned, everywhere: window ledges, étagères, once in the pocket of a hanging raincoat. Freshly brewed or brewing, Gabrielle's tea smelled like a spring garden. After it sat a while, it smelled the way flower stems look when you pull them out of week-old water.

Not too far from the herb teas was a stack of popcorn Gail had to have when we watched old movies together on the VCR. Two or three boxes of Familia left over from breakfasts with Barbara. Girl Scout cookies that were Sandy's.

Non-alcoholic champagne which Linda brought for our first (and, as it turned out, last) dinner together, about an inch-and-a-half of it remaining in the bottle.

Caviar bought for someone. (I threw the Brie away before it came after me. It had begun to glow with intelligence and ambition.)

Sardines for —

Sardines?

However desperate I became, surely I would never go with a woman who ate sardines.

Anyway, you get the idea. I'd become The Grocer of Unrequited Love.

What I did was, I contacted a food bank and donated it all.

They came by, had a look, and called for another truck. When the bombs fall, at least we won't starve: we can squat in the ruins and dine on diet chocolate soda, sardines and Girl Scout cookies as we watch fingernails grow through the backs of our hands.

At any rate, now, at last, I am truly alone here. The cabinets groan with emptiness.

2.

I want to add this: it's not *nearly* as bad as it used to be.

In 1970, for instance. That year, in the same week, I'd published my first book and ended my first marriage. Christmas dinner occurred at a Burger King just off St. Charles in New Orleans. There were three of us scattered about the room, and one of us (I'm reasonably sure it wasn't I) kept pulling napkins out of the dispenser and chewing them up. I went home and for company, as people living by themselves will do, turned on the TV. Mac Davis was singing "Drinking Christmas Dinner Alone." Listen, I told myself: they're playing our song.

This morning, twenty years later, I go to La Madeleine, where even the sparrows begging food at the tables outside are in pairs.

A student of mine once pointed out (you'd think writers would notice these things, but we seldom do) that every one of my best stories, those I most admired and those favored by readers, was a love story.

I thought: Of course. And began to consider how very sensitive I was, how sensuous and caring, how passionate, how —

The women always leave you, he said.

This year, still, is something of a landmark. One romance cancelled in January, a mid-season replacement begun in April and concluded in May when, on the second day of a weeklong trip to New Orleans, I asked where she wanted to eat that night and she said, "At home."

Camus wrote that scientists, trying to explain the world, are reduced finally to poetry, and I want to turn the tables here by observing that love for me has been rather like the speed of light: one approaches it at ever greater velocities, yet never attains it. Certain physical changes occur in the speeding object, a kind of concentration or *rendering* (as we say of fine sauces and horse's hooves).

And finally, my favorite bedtime story.

In the Arizona desert there's a curious creature called the spadefoot toad. For a year or more this hopeless romantic abides, buried beneath the parched, cracking surface, waiting for rain. And when finally that rain comes, he plunges headlong into daylight and dashes for the nearest pool of water. Here he begins sending out frantic calls. If he does not mate on the first night, he may never mate at all; by morning the water will be dwindling, and his life with it.

Sitting here now, I can't help but reflect how dry and hot it's been these past weeks. And

looking out I see — tentatively at first, a slap or two
at the window, a flurry of steps across the drive,
then a breakneck fall — that it's begun to rain.

Literary Life

One of the toughest things about being a serious writer — I mean, I can handle poverty, not being read, and checks endlessly "in the mail" — is the reputation you get, the rumors that start up for no good reason.

For instance, it is generally believed among friends, other writers and editors, that I am sorrowful and despairing. This is untrue. I distinctly remember being happy for almost five minutes in the winter of 1976, and though I cannot now recall the exact source of that happiness, I remember the emotion well, as I first took it for the onset of flu.

One critic went so far as to write of my first collection of short stories that I was "sunk in the gloom of the very young." He died not long after writing this (of course, I suggest no causal relationship), but were he still here, would have to admit that I've lived up to my early promise, having progressed smoothly and seamlessly into the gloom of the middle-aged.

Nor, I must insist, am I reclusive. That none of my editors has ever met me, that there are no pictures on my books, that even writers in my own city know nothing of me — this is purely by chance. I am very busy, and ugly. I do *not* lunch only with Thomas Pynchon (for your information, he never eats lunch) and J. D. Salinger. And I go to a party every year, though I still can't quite get the hang of it.

There have also been unwarranted charges of modernism. Freely I admit that I frequently travel from A to C in a story without so much as spitting on B. However, this is not so much choice as basic survival; I've tried writing straight narrative, and always wake up with my head on the humming typewriter. It's also been said that I leave off the endings. Believe me, if I *knew* the endings, they'd be there. Write them yourself, if it bothers you. There's usually some extra space at the bottom of the page.

(Perhaps two of the reasons I don't go to parties are the usual responses to "I'm a writer": "What do you write?" and "How interesting!" I never admit to it anymore, actually, and attempt to pass as a mortician or environmentalist.)

The loneliest profession, they call it. But two, often three times a day I stroll over to the local post office with my stacks of outgoing and incoming envelopes which all have to be weighed separately and pass the time of day with friendly postal clerks. We spend hours together.

Every day I receive letters that say, You write so well, so beautifully. And every day I send letters that say, Where is my money? Just this morning I got a check for ten dollars — for a poem I spent almost two full days writing. Words are cheap, I guess. Another batch of poems was returned after being kept for eighteen months. "Simultaneous submissions are unethical," yet another editor informed me.

Obviously I have a good life, and eat *almost* every day, and really don't mind the evictions (a new place is new inspiration, right?), so I really don't know how all these rumors about gloom and despondency got started. Except for the photos of Holocaust victims (the colors go great with my couch) and the sampler embroidered with these lines of Corbière —

> By the black stream perverted poets
> Fish, using their empty skulls for worm-pots

— I'm a light-hearted, fun guy.

Poetry: A Beginner's Manual

It's all well and good being a poet, they tell you, but what do you do with the other twenty-three hours of the day?

Of course, that's more or less in the job description: not having to worry about things like paying bills, meeting responsibilities, being anywhere on time, answering mail, going to dentists and so on. Still, the day gets long. One can only watch *A Fine Madness* or *Reuben, Reuben* on VCR so many times.

꒥

Among the most popular responses to the challenge, traditionally, has been drinking. It's rather expected, after all, and it definitely telescopes those hours. One problem with this is that you tend to wake at three or four in the morning miserably alone with *those* empty hours, the emptiest of all, staring you down.

The second most common option is phil-andering. Again, it does fill the hours, especially as one becomes entangled in the inevitable misdirection, endless *rapprochement* and creeping romance. An advantage here is that, as poets, we can get tremendous mileage out of affairs of the heart and other body parts. One *dis*advantage is that, if you're entertaining the first option, you don't have much energy (or, possibly, aptitude) left for this one. And it does require energy.

In recent years, teaching has been gaining ground as a third, albeit considerably less reputable, option.

⹌

Of course, one can always avoid the problem entirely by getting oneself shot to death in a duel like Pushkin, drowning like Shelley, being killed like Lorca by fascists, giving poetry up altogether for Abyssinian gunrunning like Rimbaud, or becoming splendidly mad like Christopher Smart.

Poetry is nothing if it's not possibility.

⹌

The secret of being a poet — now listen closely, because this is all it takes, never before revealed to the general public, a kind of guild secret — lies in putting things into envelopes and spending a lot of money on postage. It's simple percentages: the more you keep *out there*, the better your chances. (Of course, a lot will be lost in the mail and many of the magazines will fold before your contribution gets there, or while it's there, or before it appears, but this can't be helped.) Try to keep at least 300 poems in the mail at all times, more if you can afford it. Eventually, some will be *taken*. (This seems to be the word preferred by most practicing poets. *Bought* has a nice ring to it but is, alas, quite laughable.)

＄

WHAT TO WEAR. Always strive, in personal attire, to be five years behind or a year ahead of prevailing fashion, or if possible (and this is decreasingly so, with so many of us abroad), on some sidetrack altogether untraveled by others. Be advised that this may require frequent visits to thrift shops, coat racks at fast-food restaurants, bus station lost-and-founds, basements whose windows are left open or, all else failing, costume renteries. If wearing more formal attire, suits or sportcoats or the like, always sleep in the outfit before taking it into public; if dress is casual, such as jeans and T-shirt or denim workshirt, sharply pressed creases and medium starch add a nice touch. Wearing the same thing at all times is one obvious, but effective, ploy.

＄

PETS. No dogs. Cats are a terrible cliche unless over a hundred pounds or numbering in excess of thirty. (This figure is for apartment dwellers only, of course.) Aardvarks and dead birds have been enjoying a decided popularity of late. One can't top Rosetti's garden full of wombats, tree sloths and koalas anyway, so why try.

⍈

PERFORMANCE RITES. In your new career as poet, sooner or later you will be called upon, or will finally succeed in so forcing yourself upon someone that he will allow you, to read *from your work*. (And that is the way you must put it, never "my poetry" or "a bouquet of poetic musings" or "some stuff.") Remember that delivery isn't important: people *expect* you to be ineffectual (you're a *poet*, after all), and mumbling, reading the same poem four times or dropping books and papers will only confirm their expectations — the performer gives his audience what it wants! — and charm them. Perhaps the most urgent advice any veteran poetry reader can give you here is this: ignore the snoring and shuffling feet, learn a few devastating one-liners for hecklers, and always find out where the backdoor is before you go on.

⍈

FAME. "Poets console us," Apollinaire wrote, "for the loose words that pile up on earth and unleash catastrophes."

One of those catastrophes is that *everyone* — Aunt Giselle, the stockboy at Safeway, your dentist — writes, has written, or knows someone who writes poetry, and will insist upon talking about it ceaselessly the very moment he discovers your vocation. In unknown company, generally I attempt to pass myself off as someone harmless, a munitions expert or economist, for example, and at the first mention of poetry break for the (previously located) backdoor.

⁀

ELEMENTS OF BIOGRAPHY. Either eat everything in sight or live off only hazelnuts. Appear at every possible party or have it put about that you've not been seen in person in over ten years and may not, in fact, exist. You'll find that a passion for offbeat subjects — Gnosticism, say, or the Russian castration cults, or Parcheesi, about which you must speak at every conceivable opportunity — greatly enhances your image.

Remember: Poems are the product, but *you* are the package, and to sell the first, the second must become instantly recognizable.

Dentists, munitions experts, extravagant drunks or poets, we are Americans, after all, merchants and dreamers *above* all — and poetry is nothing if it's not *possibility*.

HEARTS OF THE CITY

WANDA

There was something special inside her, she told me, something she'd do or become maybe. She'd always known that, even as a child. It had set her apart from others.

I went on folding sheets and towels. We were alone in the laundromat at midday. She had taken the dryer next to my own and finally, after watching me read for a while, started talking. She was twenty-six or -seven, I guess, with limp blond hair and a heart tattoo on her left arm beside the vaccination scar. She wore old jeans and a yellow T-shirt with a pocket, no shoes. Her laundry was mostly men's clothes.

At seventeen she'd married Bill and things had been real good for a while but, she didn't know, something changed, and they just couldn't get along anymore. She'd been pregnant when they split up and lost the baby just a little while after. She hadn't been able to get pregnant since then.

She'd gone with one of Bill's friends for a year or so, you know how it is, then with some guys she met at work but that didn't work out either, that never does.

Outside, it looked like rain. Birds were lined up on wires and in the building's recesses. Trees began bowing politely to one another, elegant old gentlemen.

She wanted to know if I was married and if I had any kids. Twice, I said; a daughter. You see her much? When I can. I never knew my father, she said. He left before I was big enough to remember him.

Another young woman came in. She upended her plastic basket over one of the washers and carefully poured detergent from a small mustard jar. She sat in her car smoking as she waited. A postman in shorts and headband came in and pushed mail through the slot in the office door near us. He bought a Sprite on the way out.

Doing those for a friend, she said when he'd left, nodding at the dryer. She told me she lived in the apartments up on Cooper, the ones with the airplane propeller out front. She'd been there about six months. It was okay. You a teacher or what? she said.

I told her no, that I just liked to read a lot.

Me too, she said, used to read all the time when I was a kid. But she said she didn't seem to have much time for it now.

You live alone? she asked me.

I nodded.

Me too, she said and wanted to know if I liked it.

I shrugged. Most of the time, I told her.

Yeah. Yeah, I know what you mean, she said.

The girl came in from her car to add softener and bought a package of porkskins. I was folding the last of my laundry now, stacking it back in the basket. Hers was mostly still wet.

Hey, I don't guess you'd wanta go get coffee or something would you? she said.

I told her that I'd enjoyed talking to her and really would like to, but that I had a lot to do back at the house.

Yeah, sure, she said. Well . . .My name's Wanda, she told me. It had started to rain, very lightly. It sounded like whispers from far rooms.

Bye, Wanda, I said, cradling the laundry basket against one hip. I hope it'll happen soon, I said. And at her blank look added: The special thing you're waiting for.

Oh *that*, she said, looking into the dryer. Her own clothes and those of her friend embraced one another wildly and were thrown apart. That was just something to say, she told me. You know, something to start talking about. You be careful, she said.

I told her I would.

DON

His name was Don, and he was a writer. Mind you he hadn't published very much, some short pieces in local weeklies and a couple of stories in a religious magazine, but everything he did, everywhere he went, everyone he met, gave him ideas. He kept a notebook and wrote this all down. He'd thought of himself as a writer since the sixth grade. That was when he first read Dickens, either *Great Expectations* or *Oliver Twist*, he wasn't sure. Didn't have time to read now, but that summer he'd wrapped himself into a tight ball and read almost everything Dickens wrote. His folks kept telling him to mow the yard or go see some friends, *do* something, and he'd just say, Yeah, sure, just a minute.

I ordered another drink, wondering what his eyes looked like behind the sunglasses. The bartender put a basket of popcorn on the bar in front of us and I realized that I'd stayed over into happy hour. Don was drinking tequila sours. He didn't touch the popcorn. He watched women in

the mirror behind the bar as they entered. His
hair was long and he smelled of cigarette smoke.
He spoke just a little too loudly, as people do who
are often alone.

Maybe he'd go down to Mexico where you
could live cheap and do nothing but write every
day. Up at six, a few tortillas and some coffee, hit
the typer till siesta time, then eat again and work
on into the night. Hell, just *think* how much stuff
he could turn out! Really unload his head as Dylan
said, or rack his teeming brain as someone else
(Keats, he thought) said. Damn, he'd be another
Balzac!

There was a curious mix of clientele: young
professionals in J.C. Penney suits, predatory-
looking women whose upswept hair and bright
faces put one in mind of tropical birds, others in
jogging outfits. One girl wore a halter top
composed of two red hearts. At a corner table a
couple perhaps in their sixties sat quietly, hands
barely touching beside their wineglasses, and
looked about.

Don and I were dressed similarly — jeans, shirt
open at the neck and sportcoat, not quite the
fashion these days — and I was aware of the weight
of my own notebook tugging at a pocket. We were
probably close to the same age. I wondered if he'd

had a fig tree in his backyard and fell out of it as a kid, as I did; if he'd marched on Montgomery; if he'd seen, or fled, Vietnam; what filled his days.

What do you do, he asked me after a while.

Teacher.

Of?

Music.

Ah, that condition towards which *all* art aspires . . .

Maybe, I said. I don't know. It's a job. Bills, you know.

I do indeed.

We both ate some popcorn and watched in the mirror. Before long it started to get dark outside. Don had a couple more tequila sours, I had some beers. The women in the mirror were looking a lot better. They turned on the TV behind the bar and during the breaks Don wanted to know if I'd read Flaubert, Henry James, Turgenev, Proust, Joyce. I bet as a musician you like the classics too, he said: Bach, Beethoven. I said yes and he said I thought so. Man's best moments, he told me, the true heart and soul of the race. That's what the arts are. Not like this junk, he said, nodding to the TV. Not like what you'll find in here, what these people go home to.

After a while I told Don goodbye, paid and left. There was a light rain outside and Mozart on the car radio. I went home to an empty apartment and the middle, difficult pages of a new book. Later that night I put my head down on the typewriter and wept. I still don't know who I was crying for.

RON

When I first met him he was dragging a kite in the shape of a heart across the cracked parking lot. Women liked him, he said, because he never wore polyester.

He was from Oklahoma. His name was Ron. He'd created a big company there and sold it. Now he was starting one here, and a new life. His hair looked like a bird's nest from the wind. He wore tinted glasses and skyblue leather court shoes. You want a drink? he said.

I followed him up to his apartment. It was two in the afternoon. A Peugeot bike was lashed to the railing outside. Inside, a shapeless grey cat lay in a shoebox on the window ledge and watched me come in, then turned back to the window. I've had her since I was a kid, he said; she's old and very tired. Several plants sat on the ledge alongside her.

One corner was stacked three-feet deep and neatly with books and magazines of all sizes, forming an L behind a worn armchair. Across from that was a couch piled with papers and copies of *Penthouse.* An old wooden table near the door held a computer and VDT. There was a narrow opening in the wall between kitchen and living-room, like a gunport turned on its side, and we talked through that as he mixed Margaritas and poured them into glasses etched with mathematical symbols. He used to teach math, he said.

We'd been talking a while when someone knocked. It was a pretty, athletic-looking young lady, barefoot and wearing a torn sweatshirt, shorts.

Oh, hi, Ron. I'm sorry, I didn't know you had company.

It's all right, he told her.

The thing is, I just put this humongous quiche in the oven and if I don't get help with it it's gonna be leftover city for the rest of the week. You know how it is. You put something in, then something else, and before you know it, without meaning to, you've got this Frankenstein. I thought maybe you could come over, if you want to, I mean. Save you going out for something.

Sounds good. About an hour be okay?

Great, she said. Bye then.

She was his neighbor across the hall, he told me. They ran together sometimes. She didn't work and was around during the day when almost everybody else was gone. Mostly he worked here, he told me, pointing to the computer. Went in to the office a couple times a week, usually at night.

He'd been married back in Oklahoma. Twice, to the same woman. And when it fell apart the second time he'd decided to sell everything and get out, just *go*. He wanted to know if I'd ever loved anyone, really loved them. My daughter, I said. My wife, I thought, but it hadn't worked out, I wasn't sure. He said he wasn't either. He'd never had children, and now he guessed he probably never would.

He liked Dallas, he said, but he found it a little cold and had trouble meeting people here. He didn't know, maybe everyplace was like that now. Maybe people were just growing farther and farther apart. He tried to stay busy.

We had another drink and walked out onto the balcony. Heat was rising off cars and the asphalt, bending light, changing how things looked, just as water does. I thought of Frost's poem about fire and ice, of Creeley writing that everything is water if you look long enough. Well, I'd better go, he said. You like quiche? I told him I did. I don't, he said. My wife used to fix quiche.

I saw Ron several times after that. He was often with handsome women, some of them quite striking. He never wore polyester or smiled much. The last time I saw him he told me his cat had died.

Wounds of Waiting

I sit drinking coffee and writing in my notebook and before long she comes over and sits down
by me. She's been at the other end of the counter
for quite a while, trying to talk someone there into
buying her breakfast. I hear the waitresses talking
about her among themselves. Now she wants to
know what I'm writing. She's brought her coffee
along—all someone would spring for—and asks,
in a voice just a little too loud, for a refill.

She's had eleven operations in the last four years
and been in jail eight times. Just got out this morning,
in fact. Once she was trapped in a dumpster for two
days, eating whatever she found in there.

I tell her I'm sorry.

It's the first cool morning we've had this fall,
and I'm wearing an old flannel shirt over old jeans
and boots. Everything old today. Outside, the trees
huddle together, bent over like old men telling
secrets.

Can't find a good man and can't stay away
from bad ones, that's *my* problem, she tells me.

But I really thought I'd finally done it this time. We were putting away good money, having good times. Damn, I loved that man.

In the notebook I write: *She loved him.*

Then something changes, it seems like something *always* changes, and before I know it he's having me picked up. Says I've threatened to kill him. There's a knock on the door one morning after I've got his breakfast on the table and I answer it and it's the police. They lock me up for eight days. Then they finally let me out and I go home and he's got this little redhead from work living there with him, she's even using my makeup. So I tear the damned place apart, but I'm barely out of there before a cop car pulls up. I see this doctor for maybe three minutes. Then when a hearing comes up the judge doesn't talk to me or even look at me really, he just says the doctor recommends blah, blah, blah, and I spend the next two months in a state hospital.

She asks for another refill and one of the waitresses breaks away from the others to give it to her. Will there be anything else, she wants to know. I ask my companion if she'd like breakfast. She thanks me and says she's not really hungry. Traffic begins to pick up outside.

You married? she asks after a while.

Because the real answer is too complex, I say that I am.

Your wife love you? You love her?

Again I say yes, and yes.

Yeah. I can tell that, looking at you. Any kids?

I nod. Wind outside plucks gently at the windows.

I have two little girls, she says. I don't know where they are now. I used to work two jobs to take care of them while my husband was out drinking and buying trucks. He had seven trucks in one year. Always looking for better deals. I guess he still has his trucks. *That's* what *I* have, everything I own.

She points to a pillowcase beside the chair she sat in before. It's stuffed and lumpy, tied in a loose knot at the top.

I wish I had pictures of my kids so I could show them to you, she says.

I tell her that I wish she did too.

Well, better go, I guess, find a place to stay. Be a cold night, looks like.

She retrieves her pillowcase and comes back by on her way out. It's slung over one shoulder. She pulls her hair forward over the other. It's almost to her waist.

You take care of your wife, she tells me, you hold on to her. She's lucky. You're a good man.

For a long time after she's gone the waitresses stand watching after her and talking. I look down at her coffee cup. It's almost full. There's a faint blur of lipstick on its rim.

In the notebook I write: *A good man.*

I walk home through the bright, chill morning thinking of Apollinaire: Their hearts are like doors, always doing business. I put on water for tea and, sitting by the window, write a three-page letter that I later tear up and throw away.

⁀

He asked me where I was going and I told him I didn't know.

Do any of us, he said, and I was glad I hadn't said nowhere.

Around us the bus station went on with its slumped, bustling life. It would always go on with that life, whatever happened to each of us, to all of us, to our country, our families, our individual lives. Through the windows we could see, but not feel, a bright sun.

You a drinking man? he wanted to know.

I shook my head. Not anymore.

Me too. Used to be, though. Nothing I liked better, nothing I looked forward to more than coming home to a cold pitcher of martinis.

He looked off into the crowd for a moment. Well dressed in grey suit, pink shirt and tie. Hair casually longish, carefully trimmed, salt and pepper. Altogether an unusual patron for this downtown Dallas bus station.

Going to see my son, he said. Been, I don't know, six, seven years since we were together. Now he's a college professor up there. Boy almost flunked science every year he was in school. Now he's teaching it. Anthropology. You have family?

I shook my head.

Neither does he. Married?

Another shake.

Been that way?

I nodded.

Then you probably will be again. Twice, for me. The first one, that's the one my boy's from, that was a mistake. Never should have happened. Listen, could I buy you a coffee, or a beer?

I thanked him and said no. People broke around us like stream water around lodged twigs.

Don't know when it started, or why, and I guess I never will, now. But by the third year or so, it had got so bad I couldn't help but see it. Never even knew she drank before that. Oh, she'd have a beer when we went out, some wine or champagne, but as far as I knew, that was it. This is my second wife I'm talking about. Casey, I always called her. We're still married. You sure you don't want some coffee?

I thanked him again, and again passed.

Thing is, everything about her changed when she drank. Everything. I'd come home and find her passed out on the bed, still in her robe from the night before, and she'd always been a stickler about housework. Or she'd pick me up barely able to sit up in the car, much less drive. And then there were these rages that would just go on and on sometimes. I'd try to get away from her and she'd follow me. Into the bedroom, bathroom, out into the yard, into the car. Anywhere I went. Shouting at me and slamming doors and accusing me of all sorts of things. Got where almost every night was like that.

I don't think I'm a bad man. I never had anything like that happen in my whole life, never heard of anything like it. I didn't know what to do. I loved her. It would have been a lot easier if I didn't, if I could have stopped. But I haven't been able to do that, ever.

My son thinks I'm a fool. Refuses even to talk about her. Most of our friends don't come around anymore. Can't say I blame them – you know what I mean?

I said I did and he apologized for bothering me with it all. But sometimes, he said, you just have to talk, you know. I told him I knew. A few minutes later they called his bus and, still apologizing, he trudged off towards it.

It wasn't even noon yet, and I too was alone, with no bus to catch. I walked out into sunlight and pigeons and fastfood wrappers, wearing the same jeans as now, years later, sitting here, writing this.

Something terrible had happened in America, and within the borders of my own small life as well. I had lost someone; I had met someone. I was trying to work out my feelings. I was trying to keep *having* feelings, trying not to stop. And I was trying, as I am still trying, just to understand a little about the things that happen to us, to all of us, in the awful solitude of our lives together.

꙳

His name is Powell, Mr. Powell, room 236, bed 1, and he is flat on his back, one leg suspended above him and trussed like something about to be popped into the oven. Bottles on the floor beside him bubble when he breathes. He is reciting poetry, No man is an island, and I'm thinking no one could look *more* like an island just now. He switches to

Shakespeare. Bubbles break the surface in perfect iambic pentameter.

Donne, I say to him. Then *Hamlet*.

Riiight, he says, making the most of that word too. The cauldron beside him boils with those *i*'s. Thunder, lightning, or rain: we two shall not meet again. You into poetry? he says.

I admit that I am, and we go on about our business, trying to censor from his lungs the infection that's taken up residence there. He breathes a medicinal mist and I clap along his chest and sides to loosen secretions. When he coughs, depth charges go off in the bottles.

Mr. Powell is twenty-eight years old. One week ago he woke to sudden sharp pain in his side and found an intruder leaning above him with the knife he'd just thrust into Powell's chest. Powell took after him but because the knife had collapsed a lung, quickly passed out, taking a fall that shattered one leg. Both Powell and a woman he'd just met, also stabbed and in the bedroom upstairs bleeding out, now on a respirator in ICU, had waited most of a day before help came.

Try this one, he says when we're through. He recites most of *Dover Beach*, pausing from time to time to cough. Arnold, I tell him—in many ways the first modern poem. Wonderful, he says, somehow managing to stress all three syllables. He goes on into Hardy, Browning, Tennyson, Hart Crane. I edge towards the door. Miles to go. He begins to talk cosmology.

The speed of light, he says. Of light. And yet, it takes light from that sun some nine minutes to reach us, to fall to us here, on earth.

It occurs to me that he is reciting this litany of fact, of *science*, much as he declaimed poetry. Bubbles roll in the jars beneath him. There are also in the pitch of his voice, in its cadence, unmistakable echoes of the Southern sermons we both, in our separate churches (for Mr. Powell is black), grew up alongside.

That, that delay, that waiting, is why we can never quite live in the present, Powell tells me. Why we're forever a few steps behind ourselves, stumbling in the shadows of everything we know and want to be. We're always waiting for that light to get here, you see.

Entering with meds, an R.N. gives me the opening I need. I slip from the room and go to the desk to chart Powell's treatment. Then pass on to my other patients for the day: two-pound newborns with lung disease, young women brain-damaged in car wrecks, old men incontinent of urine and feces, unable to say any of the things teeming in their brains, unable to die.

Hours later, near shift's end, I return to check Powell's oxygen. His name remains outside the door but the bed is empty, trash can beside it overflowing, bottles there bare as ruins. I feel terribly alone just then, and walk to the window. It is almost dark outside, the city's other, far towers distant and strange. Leaning my face against cold glass, I close my eyes and think of Powell: his poetry, his science, the lift of his voice, the life in his eyes. Then I open my own eyes again and begin waiting for the light to arrive.

Where I Live

Home.

It has been many things: one-room apartments in the Midwest, Dallas or Boston; three miniature rooms thickly troweled with white plaster like cake icing in the East Village; a flat just off Portobello Road in London where I fed an omnivorous electric meter, bathed in the cold, and watched people in the flat across the street, people I never saw otherwise, peering out from behind gauzy curtains.

For years I wandered about in the throes of a wholly portable life, a nomad unpredictably folding up his tent and disappearing over the horizon, lugging typewriter, files, guitar and a few books (some of which I'd written) from There to Here, resolutely living, as one friend put it, in the cracks of society. There were failed relationships, friends abandoned (as it were) in mid-sentence, makeshift furniture, unaccountable silences.

For over two years now, home has been Fort Worth, a second-floor apartment with hardwood floors and white walls off Camp Bowie where, as I write this, I sit listening to Vivaldi mandolin concerti and watching the rain turn within itself like a self-questioning mind. I live within easy distance of La Madeleine, of our three museums, of the Ridglea. A young dancer from the Fort Worth ballet lives downstairs. We meet on my stairs or balcony, one of us coming, the other going, and talk about this artistic life I'm well along in, he's at the start of.

Friends often ask why I moved to Fort Worth and what I think of it, and I suppose that, largely, I like what many others like about it: the ease of getting where you want to be, its easy democracy, the small-town feel of it. I tell them it reminds me of college towns, which I love. And that I walk more, relax more, more often have a sense of my life opening outward here.

New Orleans was the first city I made my own, and I've always loved things and places deeply marked by time, ungentle use, diversity. I play old guitars by preference and have a decided taste for Delta blues, early jazz, string band music. In literature I find increasingly that I care little for plot, for traditional values of narrative or character development, and gravitate towards those works which have at their center, at their heart, a clear, unmistakable *voice*. And I believe that Fort Worth has such a voice, a sound and cadence all its own that, more and more, I find myself falling into.

Though we rarely understand them, there are lines of force reaching forward out of our pasts. There are continuities and personal histories: memories, habits, the fictions we create for ourselves and try to live by.

I watch the beautiful, ravaged face of the woman I love as she sleeps beside me in early morning light and, in her eyes, in the ragged landscape of her face, like Yeats' Leda see broken walls, burning roofs and towers, Agamemnon dead. My hand on the gentle curve of her back seems almost to glow with a light of its own. We really *must* love one another or die. But how do we do that—and go on doing it? Our intentions always so grand that we're able to live finally, diminished survivors, in their shadow.

Home is where we retreat, where beneath the weight of a hand our body rises into light, where our hemmed-in lives grow densest. Outside now, the rain has stopped. Cajun music plays. A neighbor, walking her dog, pauses on the street to look up and wave. The postman's legs emerge from his car. From the center, from home, I watch the world gather itself back together out there.

Circles

The books on my desk, because I am writing one of my own to be called *American Solitude*, are a more coherent lot than usual. *Walden* is here, and a couple of Thoreau commentaries; May Sarton's *Journal of a Solitude*; Suzanne Gordon's *Lonely in America*; Max Picard's wonderful *World of Silence*. It's three in the morning and I am sitting here quite alone (my wife and daughter away for a week on vacation) looking at these books and thinking again, as I have thought so often these past days, how difficult it is in America to be alone, and how easy to be lonely.

I found in my yard this morning, after last night's driving rain, an overturned bird's nest, surrounded by tatters of twigs and the soaked remains of a paper towel woven into its base. I had watched this nest, a blue jay's, for weeks, seeing a head peer over its rim from time to time, looking on as the parent, from tenuous, remote branches or powerlines, chided the cats to keep their distance. I lifted the nest: it was empty. But discovered in the grass a few feet away, all beak and legs, the body of a single fledgling, dead yet inexplicably undisturbed by the cats.

In this solitude I should, by all rights and intention, be traveling at ever-increasing velocity into myself. Instead, I find myself drawn to the world. It is as though, abandoning the daily forms of my life (for I do not write at 3 a.m. when my family is here, nor do I have one meal each day at 2 or 3 in the afternoon), I have made possible new connections to the world, new bridges. And there is a pressure propelling me towards it. Yet I have spoken to no one for almost two days now; from this quiet I reenter the world sheathed in my own silence, apart from others, an observer.

On the walls of the room where I write hang dozens of old stringed instruments. Each is ravaged in its own way (weather cracks, gouges, pieces torn away, necks bowed by time, poor repair jobs, and each (mandolin, banjo, Hawaiian and classical and steel-string guitars, sitar, Dobro) has its specific anatomy. More: each has its own distinct character. Their individual sounds, the way they feel and respond as you play them, the music they elicit from the player, these are unmistakable.

Increasingly I come to the notion of all human activity — speech, music, the theory of relativity —

as metaphor. With my family away I have taken to spending the early morning hours on the patio with my tea, just sitting and watching the world gather itself back to light. After a time the kittens forget I am there and go about their business; the spider resumes his spinning in the tree beside me. The rhythms of the world are locked into our bodies. One cannot but feel himself in some part reborn with the morning: an unfolding. So many rhythms meet in us. If you pursue the world, it eludes you; if you sit, still and quiet with yourself, the world comes to you, almost as though *from* you.

But the mind also repeats the landscape, and we live today in a landscape of riddles, of what William Gaddis has called "confusion, waste and words empty of information." Because it is that time of year, I am thinking of the bomb opening over Hiroshima like a hand. People's images were burned into the walls; others saw, even through closed eyes, the bones of their arms in the red light. Some time later their skin began sloughing away, moist pink ingots that dropped off leaving mouths that would not heal. Nothing better bespeaks the discontinuity of our times. America has become so much more subtle, and inward, with its destruction. We have supplanted both the quiet finitude of periods and the comma and semicolon with their implicit sense of continuity: now everything is connected by fitful dashes.

Another thing the dawn may elicit from us is comprehension of the want, and wisdom, of ritual in our lives. Belief that the visible world is all there is, is finally an intolerable state of mind; and ritual, as Edmund Wilson said of art in his essay on Byron, "has its origin in the need to pretend that human life is something other than it is, and, in a sense, by pretending this, it succeeds to some extent in transforming it." Art, then, is ritual. Music is patently ritual. Ritual *extends us.* If I pick up a guitar to play, I am expressing my faith in certain forms, certain patterns drawn from the world, that in playing I return to the world. Witnessing the dawn I reaffirm my own place in that dawn, in all this earth's cycles.

One small ritual that has taken on a measured importance for me is that of tea. I acquired the habit several years ago while living in London, and my preparation of tea now may vary from the fairly elaborate use of a tea set handpainted with cherry blossoms (there is also a second, workaday tea set) to simply using a teabag. But always it must be set to brew just as the water blossoms to a boil. The leaves relax and unfold slowly. One thinks of tea's many forms through the years and the world: the hard bricks of old China, Japan's tea ceremony, the Russians with their samovars and glasses, syrupy Indian chai.

And so I am sitting here with my tea (as the world gathers again into morning) thinking of solitude, guitars, Siva, tides. There is no design; there are only patterns — patterns that art and ritual extend, that they elevate. "One measures a circle beginning anywhere." As well begin, then, with music, the bomb, a single life, dawn.

As I write this, the feral kitten of a cat we call Rabbit plays in the yard just beyond my window. The kitten was born elsewhere, in some abandoned shed or woodpile, and spent his first months there alone with his mother. For some time he would bolt from the yard whenever we entered it. Now he comes regularly at feeding time, and each week dares come a little closer. I suspect there will always be that wildness, that quickness in him. But it is only man that he fears.

Closer to me, a spider follows some complex, occult path along the outside of my window, proceeding by fitful turns and sidesteps.

The kitten and I fear the same thing; like the spider I am crossing fitfully a broad plain I cannot understand, without landmark or direction. It is late summer and my daughter writes from her grandparents' home in Ohio that she no longer fits in there. The wayward tides of this world break over, and in, us all: we are all at the same time sea and shore. The same blossoming dark, the same winds unfold above our heads.

And now it is morning.

American Solitude

"In America," John Butler Yeats wrote to his poet son, "they make war on solitude."

Yet one of the enduring figures in our literature and popular mythology is that of the man alone — the recluse, the rugged individualist, the loner. Cooper's Deerslayer takes to the unbroken forest not only because of his great love for it, but also to avoid encroachments of society; legend has Daniel Boone pushing westward because someone settled within a hundred miles of him. Thoreau strolls around Walden Pond and becomes our model of the man withdrawing from society's clamor to his own thoughtful company. Huckleberry Finn and Holden Caulfield alike flee "phonies" and "big deals," the imperatives of social organization. Caulfield obsessively fantasizes reclusive life with Sally in a Vermont cabin, or remaining within society, but apart from it, as a counterfeit deaf mute.

Meanwhile Ahab's moonlit bulk on deck at night underscores our final, inexorable isolation and reminds us that American fiction, taking its cue from the land itself, has largely been one of extremes, of the giant personality working out its problems in isolation.

"He had gradually succeeded in turning his private universe into a well-guarded fortress," Kosinski wrote of a character in *Pinball*, "and up to now he had kept out anyone who might disturb the peace he found there." The protagonist of DeLillo's *Great Jones Street* at the novel's beginning has withdrawn from his career as rock musician and lives in a shabby tenement, emotionless, avoiding human contact whenever possible. Rendered mute by a drug forced on him, he recovers but chooses to sustain the illusion of muteness.

Alexis de Tocqueville on the dehumanizing potential of American democracy:

> As social conditions become more equal, the number of persons increases who, although they are neither rich nor powerful enough to exercise any great influence over their fellows, have nevertheless acquired or retained sufficient education and fortune to satisfy their own wants. They owe nothing to any man, they expect nothing from any man; they acquire the habit of always considering themselves as standing alone, and they are apt to imagine that their whole destiny is in their own hands.

> Thus not only does democracy make every man forget his ancestors, but it hides his descendants and separates his contemporaries from him; it throws him back forever upon himself alone and threatens in the end to confine him entirely within the solitude of his own heart.

Retaining high regard for individual character and initiative and at the same time a spontaneous community of values, is society's fundamental problem. As de Tocqueville points out, the ultimate peril is retreat from world or society into self, solipsism instead of solitude. And it is always, of course, a fine balance.

America has failed to establish or much encourage this balance, preferring to run its society as it does its factories, each part interchangeable. Individuality, nurturing human character and potential, self-realization — these are all fine goals but (surely you understand this, Management says) impractical ones.

While casual overemphasis on the hermit-like individualism and absorption with nature in his work has obscured its actual thrust, Thoreau clearly was not so naive as to believe that the individual could by his own action turn back the onrush of American life or greatly succeed in rechanneling it. He did believe individual development the only proper aim of society; and his work became a profound reaction against the increasing submersion of the individual in oversocialized New England towns on the one hand, and on the other, the factory system's view of nature as raw product to be converted to profit. Thoreau wanted to solve the problem of living in the world, not to change it. He knew that the individual had to be more than society's cadre, and that the individual's moral sense is the only true test, the ultimate safeguard, of social institutions. For Thoreau (as for Thomas Merton many years later) solitude became a vocation, an absolute necessity for self-identification and social survival.

Certainly there's much in America that contrives to deny solitude and impede expression of individuality. Most of us don't have distinct, formed characters; instead, we go about in costumes and masks and parade particular sets of vices. We're afloat each day in a lashing sea of noise, bodies, automobiles, information. Our children learn their language, and thus their dreams and desires, from television, popular songs and movies. Still, something more than Merton's "murderous din of our materialism" seems at work here, something more sinister and powerful than Pascal's *divertissements* "which enable a man to avoid his own company for twenty-four hours a day."

For, instinctively, we flee solitude. And, sadly, American society does everything possible not only to make this evasion effortless, but to make it seem natural and desirable. Here, Deerslayer, America says, Have a beer, sit down and watch this movie with us; pretty soon you'll forget all about wanting to be by yourself out in the woods. And a week or two later we see him driving an old Chevy, with a cooler of Coors and a portable stereo in the back, heading for a Sunday afternoon at the lake.

"If a man judges a country by the quality of its entertainment, then he is a very poor man" — this from Melor Sturua, a correspondent for *Izvestia* whose dispatch to that paper one Christmas simply juxtaposed, without comment, entries from the Neiman-Marcus catalog and examples of poverty from the *New York Times'* annual 100 Neediest Cases. The merchant mentality is no less durable or insidious, no more mindful of the individual, than is the totalitarian; it's simply more subtle.

Finally it's not materialism, but what materialism unwittingly does to us, that constitutes its real danger. Believing ourselves securely amidst the world we are instead shut away from it, encircled by our chattel, outside light fading, our desperate voices reaching out as the final stones fall into place.

"The treasures of Cathay were never found,"

writes Louis Simpson:

> In this America, this wilderness
> Where the axe echoes with a lonely sound,
> The generations labor to possess
> And grave by grave we civilize the ground.

For many years I have wanted to write a story about a baby abandoned in a shopping mall who grows up, Tarzan-like, in its dark corners and crawlspaces, emerging at night to forage for leftover fast food, coming to manhood in that strange new forest. There would be glimpses of him from time to time by night watchmen or stowaways, by people wandering on distant edges of the mall late at night. Some say that he wears discarded jackets, jeans, dresses, shoes; others that he takes what he wishes from the stores at night and is always splendidly attired. He is said to have no speech. Rumors and tales proliferate. Parents warn their children of the mall monster; it will come and get them if they behave poorly. Then sightings begin in other malls.

This would not, I think, make a particularly fine story — ideas as such rarely do — but it says a great deal about contemporary American life.

Rising from the grey seas of their parking lots, filled with promise and riches, self-contained and -sufficient, our malls are nothing less than small Americas. The frontier, Joan Didion suggests, has been reinvented, and its new form is the subdivision with its suburban mall, "that new free land on which all settlers could recast their lives *tabula rasa*."

And, as always, our minds repeat the landscape.

Though clearly the path was widening even in Thoreau's time, it was in the Twenties that we picked up deadly speed. Plunging headlong towards an urban future, we were dazed: *everything* seemed in flux. The new urban prosperity, resting on mass production of consumer goods, required parallel mass consumption, and age-old traits of frugality, thrift and self-reliance were torn away from the American people by advertising and this horrible gravity of *things*. It seemed that all the landmarks by which one made one's way — community, sobriety, individual responsibility — had been swept away. We began to long for a society in which the individual could retain control of life and livelihood; where power resided in visible, accessible institutions; where such astounding wealth might somehow be equitably shared. The factory became our commanding metaphor.

Collectivism has been the usual lot of human society, with citizens living and dying in fairly stable communities and taking for granted the individual's subordination to group welfare.

Solitude, however, was built into those societies. Our own, working to render solitude undesirable and difficult, at the same time exalts a myth of individual potency and potential. Our children rarely discover the simple pleasures of learning, of pursuing trains of ideas on their own; are rarely encouraged simply to enjoy playing volleyball. Long before schooldays, they're propelled towards competition.

"The association between failure, loneliness and solitude is so strong in our culture," Suzanne Gordon writes in *Lonely in America*, "that people often find it difficult to believe that there are some who like being by themselves." Many societies exert greater pressures than does our own to mold the individual to sharply defined group roles, but within those circumscribed roles generally there remains, still, great variation. Our society offers tremendous latitude to pursue individual ends, yet checks us by so rigorously defining what is worthy and desirable that we all tend — "independently but monotonously," as Philip Slater observes in *The Pursuit of Loneliness* — to pursue the same thing in the same way.

Paul Tillich:

> Today, more intensely than in preceding periods, man is so lonely that he cannot bear solitude and he tries desperately to become part of a crowd. Everything in our world

supports him. It is a symptom of our disease that teachers and parents and the managers of public communications do everything possible to deprive us of the external conditions for solitude, the simplest aids to privacy.

George P. Elliott says that in this world, in a republic particularly, we must help one another stop in time. We have to learn not to take the patterns for our lives and selves from society, but to discover appropriate patterns for those lives, *and* for society, within ourselves. We have to learn again to question — and to listen.

"Man is better able to endure things hostile to his own nature, things that use him up, if he has the silent substance within," Max Picard writes. But, he adds, this silent substance in the western world is much endangered. We no longer move deliberately to ideas and objects; rather, they are absorbed in our own emptiness, as into a vacuum: they rush at us, swirl around us, collide with one another. And so full of *things* is the space formerly occupied by silence, we are not even aware of its loss.

Life is all conjunctions, one thing after another; and we can't let ourselves be so distracted by life's loose change. If we're to survive we must step aside, out of the world of things, away from the comforting light of our campfires.

All day today, as I write, a tree in my neighbor's yard is being dismantled branch by branch and fed to a machine that atomizes it. Every few minutes there is a rapid and terminal *zzzzit!*, always brief but sometimes longer, sometimes shorter, then a spray of pale powder.

I'm remembering a time during college years. We lived then on Iowa farmland, and one day after crating up my wife's paintings for delivery to an exhibition we discovered that we had bought far too much lumber for the task and now had, along with the expected scraps and rag-ends, an array of wood in various sizes. Sitting there in afternoon sunlight nursing beers, we decided to build a tree. It went up on a small hill in the yard, facing, across a narrow blacktop road, fields of corn and wheat. It was abstract, certainly; it was mannered and minimal; it was ragged and rather ugly — but it was indisputably a tree. We had together, in our minds, in our imaginations, by art, by ritual, returned lumber to forest.

Generation by generation, art rediscovers the necessary rituals, rediscovers what is essential to humanize us. And we have to grope towards these same recognitions in our own lives. For the individual life, like our arts, and like nothing else, has the capacity, perhaps finally an obligation, to make the world large again.

Civility

Last week a young security guard was shot three times at a local bar by a man he asked not to carry his drink outside. The man's girlfriend, already outside, handed him the gun.

I rarely get more than a half-mile from my home without becoming depressed. Cars reign in close behind and swerve around at the first near-opportunity while drivers make savage gestures into their mirrors, cross lanes recklessly on express-ways, dogfight for the closest parking space. At my daughter's school, parents pull into the mouth of the narrow drive and sit there as they slowly unload, seemingly oblivious to other cars stacking up behind them and into the street.

New neighbors have moved next door. The man spends all his time — this seems to be his only endeavor or interest — at work on a customized truck, pounding steel and racing his engine. He has replaced the old dog that everyone ignored with a young dog that everyone ignores; it barks day and night. When my wife goes into our backyard his children shout, "Look, there's that old woman!"

All these incidents are related, points on a line, and it does not seem to me at all fanciful that the child who intrudes rudely upon neighbors will later demand the highway system for his own and attempt to kill a man who tells him that he may not do what he wishes to do. The line begins at the point we abandon respect for others, simple civility. I suppose it ends in a Texas tower, on a bridge in Atlanta, at Auschwitz.

I'm not certain when civility passed from us. Though I was brought up in old traditions of courtesy, few of my peers were, and today no one seems to be: cowboys have supplanted Southern gentlemen. An archaic usage of *civility* designated "training in the humanities," and certainly one does associate courtesy with gentility, with breeding— that is, with a kind of elitism. Perhaps we are skewered on our equality, as Freud suggested in *Civilization and Its Discontents,* unwilling to exercise the forms of civility because they imply deference, an abridgement of our brash "equality."

It is hardly surprising that, in such an expand-or-expire society as ours, the individual should mirror society's profile. In *The Pursuit of Loneliness* Philip Slater writes of the difficulty a traveler has, upon returning to the States, in becoming reaccustomed to seeing people weighted down with possessions acting as if every object they didn't own were bread withheld from a starving mouth. Capitalism long ago outgrew its political origins and became simply a system for impersonal fabrication and satisfaction of appetites. Its material achievements cannot be ignored and are not contemptible; these must be balanced, however, against more recent trespasses, and the real measure of any socioeconomic system must finally lie in the quality of the individual life, in its capacity for excellence.

We are a nation of highly stimulated appetites. Many of our gravest problems derive from this constant arousal of desire for things (from Constitutional rights to everything the television, magazines and shops display) without coincident provision of means to gratify that desire. And while received wisdom holds that in freeing the individual from external restraints democracy has achieved true individualism, such freedom from authority is a lasting gain only to the degree that it fosters establishment of our own individuality. The right to express our thoughts can have meaning only insofar as we are able to have thoughts of our own. Against this, much conspires. We witness no great flourishing of individualism; instead we see the ever-increasing isolation and powerlessness of the individual in our time, what Erich Fromm describes as "a compulsive conforming in the process of which the isolated individual becomes an automaton, loses his self, and yet at the same time consciously conceives of himself as free and subject only to himself." And of course it is quite possible for people to learn to despise the system while reaping its benefits.

"Society never advances," Emerson wrote. "It recedes as fast on one side as it gains on the other." Perhaps cohesive society is no longer possible. Some combination of American democratic ideals and America's relentless capitalism seems to have shut us away from one another, as indeed de Tocqueville predicted it would, and ultimately from ourselves. Good fences still make good neighbors, but if a man has so little regard for those neighbors, how can he possibly be concerned with the faceless people of the rest of his world?

Where we once paid homage to authority with great cathedrals and massive government buildings, we now turn our efforts towards monumentalizing the self. Today's hero is what Richard Sennett has called the autonomous person, one who rages against the official order and exists in perpetual disobedient dependence, creating a society bound largely by its disaffections. It might be good to recall the derivation of *idiot* from the Greek *idiotes*, a man alone.

Perhaps we have so long looked *away* from ourselves and *at* things, we are no longer sure of our existence. Hegel suggested that we exist only when we are acknowledged. Certainly in today's sprawling bureaucracies it becomes difficult to arrive at any firm sense of one's intrinsic worth, and poor manners may indeed become a way of self-assertion, of saying I'm here, acknowledge me, like a child's acting-out; discourtesy results, too, from the ever-increasing frustration and power-lessness that, entangled in those bureaucracies, we feel daily. Yet just such a sense of self-worth is essential. Emerson tells us: "A political victory, a rise of rents, the recovery of your sick or the return of your absent friend, or some other favorable event raises your spirit, and you think good days are preparing for you. Do not believe it. Nothing can bring you peace but yourself. Nothing can bring you peace but the triumph of principles." We are speaking here of character, of the willingness to accept responsibility for one's own life, though today we often seem to mean by "character" a certain truculence or stubborn pride, a hardness, and bad manners are not only tolerated in the

American male but actively reinforced as part of his supposed maleness.

Courtesy is at once a kind of authority and a kind of imagination. To live, we make certain agreements with each other, and with ourselves. One of those agreements is that we shall try to leap the chasms that separate us from one another and, on another level, from the world in which we live. Ritual may extend us into the world or bring the world's patterns into our daily lives. Art can have us move for a time within minds quite different from our own, allow us to perceive how *these* minds leap towards the world and others. Courtesy, of course, is pure ritual, all meaningless surface—a code that tacitly acknowledges we cannot, will never, leap those chasms. Civility simultaneously keeps others at a proper, paced distance and brings us together in ceremonial kindness. Like artistic activity, civility bespeaks no fulfillment or culmination, but endless search, and it is a search that, sadly, we seem to have abandoned.

Revolutions

YOU UNDERSTAND, OF COURSE, that as artists we are committed to man's finest efforts and moments — the greatest music, the finest paintings and poems, the most penetrating philosophies. And in this light I would like to tell you about the most magnificent meal I ever had.

It was in the early Seventies, and I was living in New Orleans. The great transcendent vision of the Sixties had dimmed considerably, and we'd all (all of us Marxists, at least to a degree) wandered off onto various by-roads of American life — "living in the cracks," as one friend put it. Certainly I was fortunate, as a writer, in being a worker who controlled the means of production. However, few consumers had much use for what my little factory produced, and what did sell often went at discount prices. But I continued writing "on spec" ("without prospects," as they used to say), living chiefly off book reviews and the occasional translation or editing job, waiting for checks to arrive. Any checks, any size.

Around Christmas I was forced to concede that a crunch, a personal recession, a time of great economic challenge, was imminent. I had twenty-two dollars and small change, two dollars (and small change) of which I spent eating Christmas dinner at a Royal Castle on Clairborne among other social rejects. But two checks were due me for stories, and the thought of these checks, or more precisely their *image*, their potency (for they could come at any time), was like hope itself; and I was able to go on. I finished several new stories and articles, but there was always a lag of some months between finishing a piece and getting paid for it, assuming that I *did* get paid.

I took the patently necessary measure: I stopped eating. Lived off hot tea with milk, sometimes a piece of toast in the morning. My uncle had sent a care package of gourmet foods that year, things like imported cheese and smoked oysters, and these, closely rationed, sustained me for a time. The humor of the situation, a starving man eating gourmet foods, neither escaped nor greatly comforted me. Somehow it seemed very . . . American, very much the capitalist way.

Late January, then. I walked on the levee, along the incurving hip of the Mississippi, watching cars dash along St. Charles Avenue, looking down on crowded parking lots. At night boats would call through the heavy fog, an unearthly sound. If I had to choose a place to be penniless, it would be either New York or New Orleans. Poverty is stamped into the streets of these cities, hammered right into the sidewalks and walls. I achieved in these weeks a great insight into the working of the revolutionary mind, even conceived a plan requiring students (and all politicians) to spend six months without money or food on the streets of a large American city. I began to regard with interest the trash cans behind restaurants I passed on my ever-longer walks.

Hunger, the physiology of hunger, the bodily symptoms, had curiously enough passed, or were assuaged by tea. But a deeper hunger came to me then. It was as though the food I took into my body were a vital connection to the world. That link having been broken, I needed some other strong access else I would be sundered from it. Images of things I saw burned deeply, vividly into my memory and remained for weeks; my hearing became acute (though, I must add, sometimes unreliable, strangely editing what was heard); a simple country song would plunge me into tears. The chiming of a chain against a ship's mast one windy night precipitated an entire short story.

On February fourth, I had nineteen cents. I also had nineteen cents on February eleventh and eighteenth. No checks came, but a few new pieces were accepted for publication, fanning back to life the near-extinct spark of hope. (Payment, of course, was deferred.) I developed a decided taste for Orwell and for science fiction of an anti-establishment bent. Ideologically hungover, I prowled the streets of the Quarter or the Irish Channel, unsure whether I was a street person— just another exploited worker of the proletariat— or the self-appointed, Tolstoy-like subject of some great revolutionary experiment. I recalled Plato's having the decent good sense to banish poets from his republic.

In mid-February, without fanfare, like most revolutions, the great experiment ended. I decided to own some food.

Entering a bastion of mercantilism (the Piggly Wiggly on Carrollton) I strolled the aisles, browsing among the choices afforded me by free enterprise. (There were, for instance, eleven kinds of corn flakes.) Not that, with only nineteen cents, I *had* a lot of choices. And I knew, of course, that the workers themselves would benefit little from my purchase.

It came down to a can of beans for eighteen cents plus tax. ("Don't wrap it, I'll wear it," I almost said.) I headed home then, hardly noticing in my fever of anticipation what went on in the streets around me.

At the apartment (small, unfurnished, but with odd bits of chairs and tables liberated from wealthier, empty apartments in the dead of night) I found a knife and cut off the lid of the can and an unnecessary bit of my thumb. Slowly, with the spoon I'd used all these weeks for tea in my right hand, I walked to the window. America was out there.

The first bite was almost too much for me. I was stunned — overwhelmed. The second was the most delicious I'd ever put in my mouth. I don't remember too much about the others — they went by rather quickly — except that in all the years since, I've had no meal that tasted as good or was as satisfying.

Standing that day in New Orleans, utterly broke and without much hope of ever being otherwise, a peasant in the land of plenty, a revolutionary withdrawn behind the borders of time, I thought for a moment, just a moment, that I heard all the city's bells pealing.

GONE SO LONG

He was a tall, hawklike man who hunched about his harmonica when he played, fitting his body around it as he might a woman. In later days he took to wearing a bowler hat and houndstooth suit. He'd been over to England, he said. Had made some records there, all these young white kids coming to see him, wanting to play with him. No one in Helena believed any of it.

Whenever I'm tired, my wife points out, the accent returns. I began consciously expunging it in the ninth grade. Reading a memoir by Cornelia Otis Skinner, I came across her own revelation that the contraction of *cannot* does not rhyme with *paint*. By the time I'd reached Tulane, the accent for the most part was gone; years of living in the Midwest, in London, New York and Boston swept away what vestiges remained.

Disavowal of the accent, of course, signaled a deeper apostasy. I sat there on South Biscoe Street in Helena, Arkansas, with Mozart, Mahler or Tchaikovsky on the turntable, looking across at a

mile-long row of tarpaper shacks where black
families lived, sons of whom had been my childhood
playmates until the age of ten when without
preamble I was told it was no longer proper for
me to play with black children. Beyond those
shacks the levee rose like broad shoulders above
the Mississippi. With that music, and with books,
I was creating my own kind of levee, inventing a
life in which I would *not* be Southern, little
suspecting that forty years later I'd find myself
engaged in a series of novels about another man, a
black man, who fled, just as I had, that same South
and all it meant.

Meanwhile I'd lie propped up in bed reading
Wilde, Joyce, Sturgeon, biographies of Shelley and
Byron and Shaw, Starkie's *Rimbaud,* while all night
long from the outside speakers of a drive-in close
by at the edge of my grandfather's property spilled
songs by Ray Charles, Conway Twitty, Arthur
Alexander, Sam Cooke, Nat King Cole and Jimmy
Reed.

Grandfather, though no longer a rich man,
lived in what was nonetheless a mansion, an
enormous structure with wraparound porch,
massive entryway and wooden staircase, two-inch-
thick doors between rooms. As a boy he'd broken
his leg and, lacking access to medical care, had a

box built about the leg until it healed; all the rest of his life, Hephaestus-like, he limped. Once, sawing wood in his workshop, he cut off a fingertip and, retrieving it from a pile of sawdust, threw it to the dog — then went on with his work. When he came to see us, limping up the hill beside our kitchen window, knowing my love of books, he'd declaim for me the poetry he'd memorized as a child, long, rolling stanzas of Longfellow, Whittier, Sidney Lanier, William Cullen Bryant.

The black man I left hunched over his harmonica there at the first of this piece was Rice Miller, aka Sonny Boy Williamson. Most summer days I'd tune in to the noontime King Biscuit Hour on KFFA to hear his mournful harmonica and voice. Throughout the Thirties and Forties Helena, with its factories and farms, with juke joints like the Blue Moon Cafe, and especially with KFFA, had been a hot spot for itinerant blues singers. Everybody passed through: Roosevelt Sykes, Robert Nighthawk, Charlie Patton, Johnny Shines. Robert Johnson lived there a while. Sonny Boy was the last hurrah of that rich blues tradition.

Sonny Boy's was wild, loose music, music with a deep anger and sadness to it. The only other connection I had with this other, alternate life lay in my odd kinship with Buster Robinson, a shambling, ageless black man living with his family in a rough cabin on my grandfather's property and surviving on odd jobs. Buster was always smiling. He called me Mister Jimmie till the day he died.

These days when I teach I tell my students: Write about the things that hurt you, write about the things you don't understand.

Been gone so long, Sonny Boy sings. His harmonica fills the spaces between halting words, harmonica and voice become a single instrument. *Been so long the carpet's half faded on the floor.*

Rimbaud wrote: I inherit from my Gaulish ancestors my whitish-blue eye, my narrow skull, and my lack of skill in fighting.

So it is that Grandfather's poetry, memories of those tarpaper shacks and of Buster Robinson, Sonny Boy's music, the books I read, have combined in some manner, an unlikely raft, to bring me here, to make me the writer I am today. I go on listening to black music, go on writing about the world of a Southern black man who, like myself, fled.

One does not escape, Rimbaud says.

Taking the Stage

It's almost time to go on and Barry tells me we'll open with *Rising Sun.* You want anything? he asks. I tell him no and pour another cup of tea from my thermos — hot tea with milk: I lived in London for a while — to take onstage with me. Yeah, Barry says, coming back with a glass of hot water, lemon and honey, *Sun'*ll get their boots scootin'.

He climbs onstage, slings his guitar — a red one from the Fifties with as many buttons and toggles as a 747, none of which seem to do anything — and tries for the fifth time tonight to tune it. Don swings in behind his drum set, adjusts seat and cymbal, gives bass and snare a trial, perfunctory thump. Jim arms himself with Fender bass and nods readiness. I take my own judge-like perch behind the steel. We'll do it in G, Barry tells us. We do almost everything in G.

The club itself reminds me of the lyrics of one old country song, so small you have to go outside to change your mind. Everything smells of beer, cigarette smoke and stale bodies. (All clubs smell the same. Years later I'll open instrument cases used then and find this smell still inside them.) There are the usual pool tables in the rear, rows of stacked plastic chairs, red lights like something from an aquarium, indeed, an underwater effect to the whole thing. And always someone at the bar drinking doubles or boilermakers and managing to stay precariously, incredibly half-drunk from 5 p.m., when we set up and go off to eat, till closing time at 2 a.m.

Barry nods and Jim starts a bass riff, one of three he knows and uses interchangeably on everything we play, simply shifting position for different keys. Three measures later, Barry's guitar punches in each downbeat with full, open chords. Drums are there—have been there for some time, you realize, though you didn't hear them till now. I come in high on a single note on the steel, letting the volume pedal out slowly so the sound of it swells and builds, then coming back down, again slowly, for Barry's vocal.

I watch Barry's cowboy hat and Waylon Jennings whiskers in the stagelight, shaping my phrases around his voice, around early echoes of it in his face, around its hoarse lull and pitch.

Almost a year of my life passed like this. Days, I listened to great historical recordings—Eddie

Lang, Django Reinhart, Lonnie Johnson, Hank Garland—and worked at books and articles on music. Evenings, I taught stringed instruments privately in my home. And nights I moved for a few hours into one or another of Dallas' country music clubs, fiddle, guitar, mandolin or harmonica in hand, or sitting behind the steel with Dobro bar and fingerpicks, backing up songs I'd often never heard before, taking break after break in G.

There's much I remember of those nights: the easy camaraderie of band members, sudden deathless fans who wound up throwing up on your amplifier before the night was over, endless urine-flooded bathrooms, the gritty, unwashable feeling of mornings after, the five or six minutes some nights when everything fell into place and you *became* the music, all of you, together.

One night I climbed down from behind my steel to do CPR on a man who'd collapsed while dancing. He was freshly out of the hospital that afternoon for observation following a possible heart attack; he'd been drinking all night and was upchucking most of it by the time I got to him, sucking an estimable portion (I had little doubt) into his lungs to become bricklike bilateral pneumonias. The band went on playing as I counted 1-2-3-4-5-breathe, 1-2-3-4-5-breathe, dancers detouring around us there on the sandy dark floor. After paramedics took over, I got back onstage for a break on "Cheatin' Heart" (yes, in G), then picked up the fiddle as Barry called "Cotton-Eyed Joe." This one we did only a couple of times a night, because once you started, they wouldn't let you stop: you were in for thirty or forty minutes of an eight-bar melody, ever-accelerating, as dancers two-stepped themselves to a Cossack-like frenzy. On the other hand, the tune was good for an entire set all by itself.

Another time, setting up, I reached down and picked up something from the back of the stage. It was a human ear, severed, I found out, in a fight that had broken out the weekend before. We been lookin' for that, the club owner told me. I half expected, all night, to find it nailed up over the bar somewhere.

There was always, at every club we played, an almost gentlemanly ritual to getting paid, the kind of precise code which exists beyond need of comment or explanation, as anachronistic in that setting as would have been camels, or pterodactyls, or for that matter, correct English. Shutting down for the night with "one last song," always a slow one, we'd pack up—sometimes the whole lot, lugging speakers and amps like stevedores down ramps and heaving them up again into murderously high truckbeds, more often (for we largely repeated the same clubs) just guitars and mikes—then settle at a stageside table for a final beer and critique while Barry rode off into neon horizons to gather our spoils, returning after some time (since he was leader, *he* had to put up with the manager's nightly critique, markedly dissimilar to our own and centered chiefly around *the door* and *the bar*) to deal out poker hands of five- and ten-dollar bills.

By this time we felt a lot like that sentence you just read: everything was happening at once, all of it running together, all of us stunned and bleary and spent in ways most people never know, unable to sort anything out. And yet with the exhaustion, with this fatally tapped-out feeling, there was also an elation that would keep us up, or tossing sweatily in beds, till far past dawn, till the rest of the house, the regular world, started about its business.

Once at a new club Barry returned from his nightly jaunt to tell us that, figuring in the band's bar tab (drinks, traditionally, are free), the manager reckoned we owed him some twenty-three dollars and small change. Just like the Blues Brothers. And yes, I *have* played in clubs where the band was inside chicken wire, as well as others where we should have been.

The club we played the longest was frequented by a scowling young man in pegged black pants, leather jacket, and quantities of jewelry of the gold-chain and signet-ring sort. Belt buckle you could eat dinner off of. Lizard skin boots. He always entered the club as though wading into water, or perhaps into an expected admiration, and developed a habit of coming onstage during sets to announce fictive contests and prizes. Word was around, as word is often around in these places, that the young man had *connections.* The word was followed, whoever said it, by the same knowing look. After a week or two of this, I began getting down offstage whenever he came on, and finally told Barry to put a stop to it. At the next break the young man came over scowling and tough to tell me he had *friends,* didn't I know that, and he could have my job in a minute. Oh, I said, you play steel? As far as I know, he wasn't seen there again. A few weeks later, following an alter-cation with the manager, who wanted to bill us for his broken PA, we also left, taking wives, families and girlfriends (who often outnumbered other patrons) across the alley to a rival, smaller club.

For weeks before we formally became a band

with our first Saturday night gig, we had rehearsed in a room reminiscent of a ship's crow's nest or poet's garret, a room tucked away under some unknown fold of Barry's roof at the top of narrow, winding stairs, partially finished with scraps of plywood and woodgrain tiles and wholly unair-conditioned. That summer, every day for almost a month it was over a hundred degrees, and as we sweltered there, searching for the fabled land of music, fumbling hour after hour to tune our instruments approx-imately together and end songs likewise, buckets of iced tea were hauled up to us in a kind of fire brigade by those wives, families and girlfriends. Then one night I showed up for practice and found out we started playing at a bar in an hour. No more looking out for land from great heights. No more worry about sweat shorting my guitars out.

Like most bands, and, indeed, most human groups, we were a disparate lot. Collectively we were Choctaw, after Barry's wife, a loving, beautiful Indian crippled by arthritis and battling alcoholism. Barry himself had two or three jobs, a priceless, unplayed Martin guitar in his closet, and a lifelong dream. I just want to prove to myself that I can do it, he said over and over. (And he did, bless him. How many of us ever do? And how many bear the terrible weight of always wondering?) Our bass player, with thinning hair and shirts such as you see only in old Western movies, was easing into midlife crisis, a gentle, quiet man who sold farm machinery all week and worked as a volunteer for the sheriff's department weekends. The various drummers were into light drugs, heavy sex or drinking, bounced checks at the 7-Eleven, not showing up at all, and stealing the band's equipment when left overnight.

In many ways, though, I was the greatest misfit of all, an intellectual trying to pass in shit-kicker land, a guy who went home and listened to Mozart, Robert Johnson and Sonny Boy Williamson and then, every weekend, came and played, or tried to play, *this* stuff. Keep it country, Barry kept saying. Child of the Sixties, ex-folkie, I tried. Fresh from the coast of bottleneck guitar and Alabama blues fingerpicking, first electric instruments shakily in hand, I was like a backwoods herbal healer suddenly given scalpels and bonesaws: I was dangerous.

Certainly there was something elemental about my time with Choctaw, something like what is at the very core of the country music we played: a starkness, a yielding hardness, that grey edge of solitude and rebellion which remains, however unsightly or however disclaimed it may be sometimes, at the heart of our heritage as Americans.

Sometimes still, I find myself with face pressed against cool glass looking off into the distance as though seeking new land in this sea, this forest, of buildings. I think again then of the cowboys with feathered hats and mannered walks and trucks hitched up outside for quick getaways. I think of desperados waiting for a stagecoach that will make their fortune. And sometimes I think again about the ear we found, imagining it still there at the back of the stage, pressed to the ground, listening still, still waiting.

STANDING BY DEATH

You don't know me, but I was standing at your baby's bedside last night as we watched her die. I held a dark bag which let me breathe for her, because she couldn't, or wouldn't, while a nurse squeezed with two fingers at her failing heart. For almost two hours I stood there, forcing air into her lungs, watching as her heart rate dipped ever lower and her skin turned grey like ash or smoke, knowing it was all no use, that soon she would be gone from us. You sat beside me, doing nothing (what could you do?), knowing (I could see it in your face) the same thing.

I don't know what tracks your mind found for itself as we all watched the widening, lowering stabs of her heart, slapping her back almost to life from time to time with drugs. I suppose you must have thought of an earlier child, dead the same way, too early arrived on these shores. You must have thought about your own life, and what point it has, what purpose. Maybe you considered the name you'd picked for this child, a name that will carry almost unbearable associations now.

In the end, if we can know anything at all, we can only know ourselves, and as you sat there shut into your pain, that awful distance swelling between us all, my own life lifted its dark head across the bed and watched as I went on about my work, went on with what I do, with what (at least in part) I am.

As a child I began telling stories daily to classmates and, at home, filled page after page with plots, conversations, beginnings I could never continue, never go on with. More and more, with age, my life seems to exist to be turned into these quiet pages, into literature. People I have loved are put to rest in one or another novel or story; relationships are sorted out in poems, then abandoned, or the other way around; the deepest, most engaging and damaging moments of my life become notes, then pages and, finally, books. This is the purpose my life has taken. Maybe in the end it's only that I want to leave a mark, something to show that I've been here.

In the car this morning, going for coffee, I tell my wife about you. I tell her about heart rates and blood gases, about drugs, about the look on your face and how your husband never spoke. I don't tell her how, washing up at the sink afterwards, I cried for just a moment there in the bright lights of the NICU, or how, pulling equipment away from your baby's bedside, I looked down at her for the last time as nurses tucked her into the folds of a blanket.

We must go on, we have to find ways that will *let* us go on, whatever they are; I hope you understand this. And that is one of the uses of literature, perhaps its only use, because words know, even when we don't, that there *are* ways to go on, that there have always been, and that we pretty much all stand at the same dark bluff (like the dark face of my life watching me across your baby's bed) looking into the same featureless gorge.

And now your child has passed into that gorge. Less than a year ago, much like your baby, my wife hovered at the same bluff, slapped almost *out* of life by drugs, unknowing, as the machine beside her made her go on — as I earlier, not as husband but as therapist, bagging her, intervening, had made her go on. For a long time she did not want to go on. There are days still when she does not want to. We live always with that question, with the distance that grew between us on her visit to that other country, death. Debts have escalated steadily with unpaid bills, medical expenses, lawyer's fees. Her children have been taken from us. We have only one another, and whatever solace we can find in our work, in friends, in a sunset or the sound of locusts, in music or literature, in ourselves.

And now, on this morning two days after your baby died, as I sit looking out on traffic and gathering clouds, trying to put into words what little I know about death, what little I have learned about my own life, it becomes important to me that you understand this, though I'll never see you again: Those of us who stood there beside you that night cared. We shared with you the fading of your child's life. Because you are human, you are not alone.

Living Without History

Two were women, in their late teens perhaps, both pregnant. There was an older woman of forty or so and four children with dirty clothes and faces. The women were looking through books on childbirth. Every few seconds one would say to the others, *Oh gross!* and show them a photograph. We oughta take *this* one to show the guys, they said.

With a chill I realize that I am looking into democracy's face. *This* is Tocqueville's "great beast," the silence that spirals down from our society's incessant noise. In these small lives the French Revolution never occurred; Mozart, the Buddha and Einstein never lived. These are lives that barely escape the ground, lives covered over by what Thomas Merton called "the murderous din of our materialism."

Long ago Santayana recognized that civilization did not spring from the people but rose in their midst by variation from them. "A state composed exclusively of such workers and peasants as make up the bulk of modern nations would be an utterly barbarous state," he wrote. "Every liberal tradition would perish in it; and the rational and historic essence of patriotism itself would be lost."

Civilization, Santayana believed, could be judged only by the excellence of the typical individual life. But democracy, while implying promise of fulfillment for each life, carries also "a vulgar, anonymous tyranny" — the fetish of uniformity. And this fetish is unceasingly fed by the media, by our schools, by every arm of social pressure. So it is that largely we wind up listening to the same music, eating the same foods, reading (if we read at all) the same books, thinking the same thoughts over and over. Each day's experience repeats the previous day's; new images cannot find their way into our lives.

I have been thinking that the origins of the American dream include both a sense of God's special covenant with America *and* the Calvinist sense of lurking evil, and perhaps together these suggest that we may win what we want without sustained or concentrated effort, and that things must be taken at face value, that we shouldn't look beneath their surface.

Similarly, we are driven to achieve as much pleasure as possible for the least possible expenditure of time and effort. Only a fool would prefer two weeks or a month with *Bleak House* to an hour of *Friends*. Big is better, quick is a must, more is the American way — and we are easily distracted. Movies, TV and popular music have become the sole cultural referents for most of us, the lowest common denominators of sex and popular entertainment, to our overstimulated selves, the only real source of stimulation.

Our worlds, our lives, grow ever smaller.

Conversation, literature, letters and education today find themselves taken with, and enervated by, a consonant emphasis on the functional and purely contemporary. An inevitable mechanization of the way we live, the way we think (for the two are finally the same), results. Our young have been sundered from tradition and the entire creative heritage of their race; they live in an endless present, without illusion, without history, with only a series of images that flash across their lives and quickly fade. They are like pools of still water left behind on the beach when the tide goes out.

I looked about me there in that library, at those women yoked to their bodies, their minds revolving like great, clumsy fans inside them; at others with stacks of romance novels or mysteries; at the children staring into magazines. I remembered a story of Voltaire's. "How can you prefer," wise Ouloug asks, "senseless stories that mean nothing?" "But that is Just why we are so fond of them," the ladies reply.

What is often meant by progress is simply acquiescence to convenience, the yielding up of yet another brace of life's possibilities for the safe, the known, the brand name, the redundant. Our cities and their malls have became indistinguishable, another blur like the blur of noise that assails us endlessly.

I lived, for a time in the Sixties, in Boston, and never have I felt more in touch with this nation's history, with its weight, its presence. Almost daily I was flushed from the library there because of bomb threats. We would wait outside in the square and finally be allowed back in. Once, riding home from the library on the trolley, I saw spray-painted on the side of a 7-Eleven store: *Convenience kills!*

It does, you know. Convenience and uniformity as well. And we've become masters at both.

I thought of Boston there by those Dallas women, thought of the trolley and that long walk up the hill to where I lived. There was a woman waiting for me then, and a book I was writing. Now I am alone. I wander among laundromats and libraries, looking out at all these faces, feeling the distance between myself and others grow ever greater, feeling all our worlds grow smaller, smaller, like receding, unreachable stars.

One Sunday

Think how impossible our lives would be, my friend says, *without literature.*

Or music, I think. Yet we know, both of us, that the mass of our fellow men do live wholly without literature — without allusion, without the imaginative riches of the race. One summer I watched my daughter, age twelve, read *The World According to Garp* cover to cover. This summer a new daughter (for I have once again sidestepped into a new life) considers, daily it seems, the problem of evil. She does not know to call it that, but it is quite real to her, actual, not abstraction. Nine years old, she is desperate for order.

For a long time I lived alone in the company of books and records. Went for days at the time without speaking to anyone but postal or library clerks. Watched women drop their children off at the daycare center opposite me. Read Voltaire and Canetti, ate leftover curry and cucumbers off a newspaper spread on the desk.

Saturday at the library I came across a girl of perhaps fifteen. Wild-eyed, she looked about at the shelves looming like ancient tall trees over her; spoke to herself; finally asked a librarian to help her find "the part of the building where Sarah D—" was. Her request was indecipherable, and with every repetition she grew more frantic.

The new apartment where I live is inhabited by roaches. They are ineradicable and overrun everything. "Ralph and his family," we refer to them. Yet there is about them something truly elemental; they are liquid, mobile slivers of time, fragments of the lost past, of a covert future, quick splinters of night and final darkness: they both repel and attract us. Unlike the girl, these roaches know no alien ground. They drift across my books, the kitchen table, piles of manuscripts, cutlery in drawers, teacups, letters. Like time itself, touching everything.

We are sitting outdoors, my friend and I, under the eave of a small restaurant's timber roof, half-full glasses of wine before us. Years ago we played together in a country band. He has gone on into a Ph.D. and teaching; his poems still appear infrequently in the literary magazines. Like myself he has married again, a younger woman. He seems to spend a lot of time at things like faculty weenie roasts. He is certain that he knows what makes a good poem, what makes a piece of writing *work*.

Years ago I also taught, certain that I passed on select tools, precious insight, to my writing students. The truth is that I did not know what I was doing, and this has become clearer with passing years. I read old poems and stories of mine and they are like things dredged from the sea, secret and mysterious. I find that I can only work by intuition and have no interest in writing when I know where the text will go.

We leave and walk along past used-clothing stores, specialty grocers, a collectors' bookshop. My friend tells me about his new wife, a nurse. I talk about what I am writing at the moment. He says: *You are still alone, then, with your words.*

And I suppose that I am.

The apartment is empty when I return, wife and daughters at the pool. A bag of groceries, bent to one side like an old boot, sits on the counter. I hear far off the drudge of traffic, the chitter of children, and I stand for what seems a long time at the window, poised like a moth at the sill, before I reenter this world. I remember Creeley: love is a process like decompression for the diver.

Just as I cannot see how an accumulation of moments can comprise a life, yield any order, I've no idea how these fragments — the girl at the library, daughters, a new apartment, roaches, writing — add up to an essay, to a piece. I have only the intuition that they might, and scribble them down in the back of a notebook.

Outside my wife stands with sunlight behind her, face poised from old habit, waiting for the moment's mood. Then she shrugs away history and smiles, tells me about her day.

How'd it go with David, she wants to know. He took the divorce hard, she knows, though she has not met him. *How is he?*

He's fine, I tell her. I lie down beside her, staring up at the bright sun, everything blanching out, on its way to becoming simpler, pure. *We're all going to be fine,* I say.

Temporary Life

This happened some years ago: on March 6, a few days after her thirtieth birthday, my wife took a massive overdose of the medication given her for depression.

We had been married less than a year then, since May. The last months had been difficult ones as I pressed her to seek help and she denied needing it. There were sudden rages, long periods of withdrawal, a bottomless sorrow.

Kim was brought to the hospital where I served as chief respiratory therapist. For almost three hours we pumped her stomach, flushed her full of charcoal and Ipecac, resuscitated her. She was having terrible seizures and required huge doses of Dilantin. She had almost stopped breathing. The medication she took, we all knew, often leads to brain damage, kidney shutdown, cardiac dysfunction.

I held the mask over her face, leaned close and spoke to her the whole time as I breathed for her. She remembers none of this. I will never forget it.

At last she was stable and we rolled her along the corridor, out into bright, bright sunshine to the waiting helicopter. Kim rose with a mighty heave into the sky. It was a three-hour drive and I didn't know if she'd be alive when I got there. I had to clean up, see to the girls, pack Kim's things. I looked down and saw charcoal all over my tie, shirt, pants. There was blood, too, not a lot of it, but it was Kim's blood. The director of nurses made me drink a cup of coffee. It kept spilling into the saucer.

⁓

The first time I wrote about her was in an essay on death published in the *Star-Telegram* not long after we met. There would be others later on—"Standing by Death" as the gulfs between us grew, and finally, when Kim was gone, gone at last after many rehearsals, "Old Story at Airport"—but much about that first essay now seems prophetic.

I watched three people die today, it began. Then went on: It is something I have been doing for a long time now, something one does not want to become good at, but does. One signs off the chart, gathers up equipment, walks away.

On my thirtieth birthday a fist closed inside my father's chest and he fell to the floor. Almost without thought I started CPR, and the world came slowly back to his eyes. But it was a much smaller world than the one he'd left. For almost a year we watched him hunt empty fields, sniffing at the stillness, disability, pills, his days like birds forever suspended in mid-flight against the morning sky. After several practice runs, at the end of an afternoon spent in a lawnchair in the sun watching me mow the yard, he at last left us.

Tonight, as the moon buoys in and out of clouds, I have lain awake thinking of all the others.

The first I remember is Mr. Sheldon, dying of emphysema. For almost thirty years he had carried in his wallet a tattered pay stub from the week he'd made over a thousand dollars operating heavy equipment, and showed it to me late one night in his room.

Mr. Petrie, a bus driver whose lungs blew up like stiff balloons and burst. The newborns I've worked with for so long now. Debbie. And the other kids — cystics, surgery patients gone sour, Siamese twins, chronic hearts — each with his own private battle pitched, and going on invisibly, above the bed.

An hour or so ago, unable to sleep, I walked to the corner store for a paper. A nearby house stood burned out in the moonlight, car after car reversing or slowing to look at it. For months, walking by, I had watched the woman and the children who lived there, wondering about them, what their lives were like, what things might be important to them.

Lately, they'd not been around very often. I'd see the car in the driveway some days, and once or twice a week old newspapers got collected from the front yard. I supposed that some great change had occurred in their lives.

So many things crowded into my mind as I walked. I remembered a poem of Edna St. Vincent Millay's: "I shall die, but that is all that I shall do for death." I thought of the knight's wife in *The Seventh Seal* saying to Death: "You are welcome in this house, Sir." Of Dylan Thomas' "Do Not Go Gentle" and "If My Head Hurt a Hair's Foot," a dialogue between mother and fetus. Of Camus, that there is only one imperative: to come to terms with death, after which all things are possible.

Back home, I lay staring at the moon's pale, round face. Clouds the shape of a piano, of Brazil, of a fig, crossed it. Winds nudged at the side of the house. I fell asleep, death's first degree, that daily rehearsal.

Six weeks have passed *(I wrote)* since the above words were put down. As often occurs, there was a space between the beginnings of a piece and its end; these words waited in a file until I came back to them. I always do come back, sometimes after moments, sometimes years.

There have been other deaths in these weeks. As I write, a twenty-two-year-old woman daily loses ground in ICU. In the other ICU, for newborns, a twenty-five week baby struggles for life. I stand over him thinking what a sense of loss these children must have, obtaining the world.

Almost daily I walk by the burned-out house.

On the day I watched three people die, I went out for the first time with a woman I had watched across many rooms. She told me of a man she had loved who killed himself. I had no idea, writing of death later that night, how important she would become to me, how in later weeks my days would gather around her troubled face or smile.

It's a warm, windy afternoon and she'll be over soon, after work. I have been defrosting my refrigerator, and something about that—the slaking of ice, unfolding the ice's lie, its whiteness—seems appropriate.

As a child, I fell from a fig tree. The world went away, and I could not breathe. For what seemed a long time I existed in a kind of limbo, not breathing (and so not quite fully alive), senses poised but blank. Like moonlight, like ice, I was white, I was pure, in that moment before the world reclaimed me. I had then, I think, my first sense of how terrible and difficult endings are.

⌒

When I wrote that, I was living in a garage apartment in Arlington, Texas, not far from the hospital where Kim and I worked; many days I'd walk over. I spent hours walking all *over* Arlington, hours more watching squirrels out the window, the remainder of my free time writing. I was writing at a fairly speedy clip: a novel in a little over a month, a dozen or so stories and articles, new poems. I'd no expectations of ever being other than alone and had given up dating. I'd just go on writing, working, listening to Mozart and Mahler, walking, running. Martinis at night as I read.

Then Kim came into my life, like a nail into cork.

Everything had always been difficult for her — childhood, previous marriages, parental relations — and as I got to know her (or thought I did), I thought I would be able to make it all easier, I began to want to.

We just met incidentally at work, at first. In the halls or cafeteria line, at various nurse's stations, in ICU when we were both assigned there. We began to talk, a little more each time, coming to recognize our common attraction. Then one day I asked her to have lunch with me and, after lunch, walking back to the unit, dinner the next evening. *Yes.* For hours that afternoon, gravity lost any claim it had on me.

I was forty, Kim twenty-nine.

When I picked her up that first evening I was stunned, stunned as I have been ever since, by her beauty, by the life in her eyes, the gentle ease of her body, by the way her mouth shapes itself around words. As we swung out onto 1-30 for the drive to Dallas, everything about me — my writing, my books, age, prior marriage, study of French and Russian, longtime work as a musician — came out in a sudden rush. Kim was quiet for a while then. She crossed her legs, tucking her feet under her, and looked off towards Dallas, towards Reunion Tower. "There's nothing to tell you about *me*," she said.

I looked at her and felt something changing inside me: borders or walls going down.

There turned out to be, once we settled in at The Wok, quite a lot to tell me. For almost two hours Kim talked about her life. The man she'd loved who killed himself, her first marriage at fifteen, a history of offbeat illnesses going back to infancy; things she treasured and things that broke her heart, her mother's debilitating illness, daughters Carey and Katie; and that all she'd ever wanted was someone to love her, someone *she* could love, someone who wouldn't *change* on her.

When I got home that night, I wrote her a brief note on stationery from DMFA's Bonnard exhibit. In forty years I had never felt these things for anyone, never known anything of this intensity, and I tried to restrain myself: I was afraid.

⁀

In the one-room apartment to which I retreated from the one we shared, I looked over Arlington, the lights and evening bustle, and I thought: I am again alone, wholly alone, as I was before Kim. I knew early on that there was a deep, irredeemable wound in my wife, some dwelling hurt that might swell and swell till it overcame her. And I knew, I think, that our marriage would not survive that wound.

I waited for her feet on the stairs, for her letters, waited to open the door and find her there. I got up every few minutes and looked down into the parking lot.

⁀

Today it rained everywhere in the world, Kim. I sat in the new apartment watching it come down, blurring the contours of our world, softening, healing. Earlier I had walked for an hour or more in the park, following Marrow Bone Spring alongside which Indians once lived, now almost dry and choked with rotting vegetation and the detritus (soft-drink cans, cigarette packages, plastic wrappers, paper) of our civilization. Birds and living, stirring things everywhere, except inside me.

Returning, I passed the Confederate cemetery we never visited but meant to, thinking that the first time I wrote about you was in an essay on death and dying.

I've been thinking a lot about pain today.

About the pain in your eyes that morning when you woke on the ventilator and turned them towards me. *I hurt,* you wrote. You had hurt a long time, hurt horribly, and I had never known how much, never suspected.

I've been thinking how something further broke within you with each hospitalization. And of all the pain of these final weeks, when you began to turn your hurt and anger out towards me, preparing to leave, but having to do that first in order to.

I waited on the edge of your life, obscured by your pain and preoccupations, reduced at last to

nurse and parent, to movies at two in the morning
and morning drinking. We had been so proud, right
up to the end, of our sexuality together; and when
that went, when you could focus only on your need,
I knew it was over.

I've also been thinking of your seizures in ER,
those great shudders as though death were already
violating you horribly. About the scars and bruises
that riddled your body for weeks afterwards.

But finally there's no moral to a near-death, Kim,
just as there's none to this rain, to a morning walk
along a spring, or to terrible, difficult endings. They
happen and we survive them, finally. We go on.

Gradually you stopped caring. Clothes were
removed and thrown on the floor where they
stayed. The bed remained unmade. I cooked all
meals, did all cleaning. You put makeup on only
when we went out, and instead of brushing your
teeth, ate toothpaste. Then you lost all taste for
food and for days ate nothing. I found lipstick on
the gin bottle's mouth. When I came home you
were always on the couch face down, half-nude.

Now you are elsewhere, in some other house,
one not burned-out perhaps, and I have my own
pain and terrible anger to deal with, to survive.

Your first weekend out of ICU I visited, sitting
with you for hours on plastic chairs beside heaped

ashtrays at the end of the hall, pigeons looking in at us from beyond locked windows. The following weekend they gave you an overnight pass and we spent it in restaurants, bars, a cheap motel room, holding one another mostly, looking into one another's eyes and talking, trying to rekindle kindness, concern, love.

I think about how we felt that weekend, Kim, how you could hardly speak from having had the tube in your throat, about the way your back hurt and the sadness and surrender that's never since left your eyes. Maybe it was always there.

It goes on raining.

≈

Returning to the house after it was all over, that first part of it, ER, court, telling the girls, to hurriedly pack things for you, hoping you'd need them.

Breakfast dishes were piled on the counter, drawers and cabinets stood open. A saucer with the birthday cake Melba brought you was on the table. A few bites had been eaten; much of the rest was smeared across the table's surface and edge. A fork lay on the floor alongside, encrusted with icing. There were pill wrappers everywhere.

With even greater dread I walked to the bedroom. Peaceful and orderly here, just a blanket pulled onto the floor, phone on the bed, your clothes spread about on bureau and chair. It doesn't look at all like a place someone's life almost ended. There's no real sign of the pressures, of the crushing pain and turmoil you went through just hours ago here.

How could anything so terrible, so devastating, I think, leave so little wreckage in its wake?

⁍

Damaged though she was, you have to understand this, Kim made me part of humanity again. Taught me to feel, to care deeply, to turn loose and give up myself. And so in her months of need I flooded her with letters, poems, stories, notes. I thought words could fix her, words could repair the damage, bridge the gulfs opening between us. I've always believed too much in words.

And much as I did, *just* as I did, all of you are waiting for the expository lump, for the part of the movie where some eccentric genius comes on to explain it all away: to tell us why things have got to be the way they are, and how, with the employ of his rare understanding and arcane science, they will be set back in order by movie's end.

As we went from facility to facility, from crisis to crisis, each one more bleak and damning than the last, *I* waited for explanations, for magic pills or words, for some god (wearing a white labcoat, of course) to descend from the cyclorama and tell us what to do. I knew better, of course. But I *loved* her, you see: that's what this is all about.

So you won't find explanations and a tidy case history here, because I don't know; no one knows. All you can expect from this accounting is a scrapbook, a collage, bits and pieces — because that is what our life together was.

Somehow Kim never learned to act, only to react. Her entire life was a passing parade of improvisations, of momentary coping in which truth, often in the same conversation, took on quite different masks. Speech and action grew ever more dichotomous, and her focus, her attention, was tugged a hundred ways at once. I managed to keep her up, keep her afloat, for a while, but when *my* energies were expended, we both almost went under.

Sartre tells us that life is the reworking of a destiny by a freedom. For Kim, all her life, there was only a destiny. She couldn't break through to the freedom, couldn't find it, couldn't believe in it.

⌒

It's four in the morning and the untidy pile of manuscript beside me is almost done now. Beer cans litter the apartment. I am playing country music because that, too, is part of Kim, part of our life together. A thick folder of her letters and notes, of mine to her, of souvenirs retrieved from unlikely places, cardboard boxes and the back corners of drawers, lies on the floor beside me. There's no desk or table in the new apartment and I'm sitting on the foot of the bed with an end table pulled up to me, typewriter and dim lamp on that. This is how I've lived my life: with these departures and partial retrievals, alone with words in new apartments in many early mornings.

～

This all happened years ago.

In *this* early morning, in my bare apartment, in Texas half-light with the smell of magnolia and tomorrow's rain lofting in from outside, I take out an old manuscript and read it through, making changes as I go, adding words or phrases, deleting whole paragraphs: *this* manuscript.

I have gone on to another life, and from these calmer ports am trying again, as I tried then through storms of sentiment and anger, to understand.

Day puts itself together outside my window, finding me not at all surprised that I don't understand much better than before. And while anger and pain remain, sadly I can recall now little of the joy or good times, little of that love I felt so strongly, save what I've put down here — reason enough, surely, to send this story, after all this time, into the world.

About the Author

In a career spanning some thirty-five years, James Sallis has produced twenty-two books and hundreds of shorter pieces. His work includes poetry, translation, essays, reviews and criticism, musicology, science fiction, and mysteries. Recent and forthcoming books include a biography of Chester Himes, a major collection of poems, a two-volume *Collected Stories*, a new edition of his book on noir writers, *Difficult Lives*, the first paperback publication of his acclaimed translation of Raymond Queneau's *Saint Glinglin*, and paperbacks of his own two most recent novels.